"Boards have never been under more pressure to provide o
the most vigilant board members can be blind to relationsh
really going on is a constant challenge. This book is a wor.
boards to develop better ways to collaborate, challenge and converge on strategies to guide
them through uncharted futures."

Margaret Heffernan, CEO and Author *Wilful Blindness*

"There's a very fine line between boards where the sum of the parts adds up to materi-
ally more than the individuals, and those with real and fundamental issues. Small changes
can result in big differences, but spotting what to change and knowing how to change it
isn't easy. This book brings some real science to this topic, as well as sharing the authors'
extensive experience to help us make sure we live on the right side of that very fine line."

Jeff Dodds, Virgin Media O2's Chief Operating Officer, Charity
and Public Sector Non-Executive Director

"*The Secret Life of Boards* is grounded in psychological and neuroscientific knowledge,
real life stories and case studies from board members and plenty of practical, simple, yet
powerful tools and strategies. This is a valuable resource for any board member and is also
a very interesting read!"

Tracy Sinclair, MCC, International Coaching Federation, Global
Board Past Chair

The Art and Psychology of Board Relationships

The relationships within boards can make or break an organisation, but well-functioning relationships take skill and effort to maintain. This book looks at the psychology behind individual and group behaviour and offers tactics and power tools to help make a success of your board career.

The book shares advice and practical tips from 40 experienced board members from the worlds of corporates, the public sector and charities on how to spot and manage complex dynamics. And each chapter ends with techniques for unlocking tricky board relationships that you can put into practice immediately. The authors examine case studies and explore topics such as psychodynamics, cognitive behavioural psychology and neuroscience for insights into how boards react under pressure. They then demonstrate how to practise the ART of managing board relationships by increasing Awareness, Relating constructively to others, and choosing Tactics to ease tensions and foster collaboration.

The Art and Psychology of Board Relationships: The Secret Life of Boards reveals why board relationships lie at the heart of organisational success – and how you can use them to gain competitive edge. It is essential reading for current and aspiring board members, coaches, facilitators and anyone with an interest in boardroom dynamics.

Joy Harcup is an executive coach with 20 years' experience working with clients in the FTSE 100, public and not-for-profit sectors. A former lawyer specialising in dispute resolution, she has an MBA from Bath University. Joy was President of the UK Board of the International Coaching Federation, the largest global professional body for coaches.

Helen Hopper trained in management consultancy with Accenture, and in occupational psychology with SHL, before co-founding leadership consulting firm h3 in 2010, where she is a Partner. She has degrees in Politics, Philosophy and Economics (Oxford University), and in Psychology (The Open University). She is an active supporter of mental health charities, most recently as COO of The Listening Place, and Trustee at The Mix.

The Art and Psychology of Board Relationships

The Secret Life of Boards

Joy Harcup and Helen Hopper

Routledge
Taylor & Francis Group

LONDON AND NEW YORK

Designed cover image: © Getty Images

First published 2024
by Informa Law from Routledge
4 Park Square, Milton Park, Abingdon, Oxon OX14 4RN

and by Informa Law from Routledge
605 Third Avenue, New York, NY 10158

Informa Law from Routledge is an imprint of the Taylor & Francis Group, an informa business

British Library Cataloguing-in-Publication Data
A catalogue record for this book is available from the British Library

Library of Congress Cataloging-in-Publication Data
Names: Harcup, Joy, author. | Hopper, Helen (Leadership consultant), author.
Title: The art and psychology of board relationships : the secret life of boards / Joy Harcup, Helen Hopper.
Description: Abingdon, Oxon; New York, NY: Routledge, 2024. | Includes bibliographical references and index. | Provided by publisher.
Identifiers: LCCN 2023015073 (print) | LCCN 2023015074 (ebook) | ISBN 9780367355586 (hardback) | ISBN 9780367355593 (paperback) | ISBN 9780429340239 (ebook)
Subjects: LCSH: Boards of directors. | Interpersonal relations. | Interpersonal communication.
Classification: LCC HD2745 .H37 2024 (print) | LCC HD2745 (ebook) | DDC 658.4/22–dc23/eng/20230406
LC record available at https://lccn.loc.gov/2023015073
LC ebook record available at https://lccn.loc.gov/2023015074

ISBN: 978-0-367-35558-6 (hbk)
ISBN: 978-0-367-35559-3 (pbk)
ISBN: 978-0-429-34023-9 (ebk)

DOI: 10.4324/9780429340239

Typeset in Times New Roman
by Deanta Global Publishing Services, Chennai, India

In loving memory of Hugh, described by colleagues as "a consensual engineer" and always my inspiration. Joy

In deep gratitude to Stuart, ever constant source of support, stimulation and surprise. Helen

Contents

Preface

Some years ago, we were invited to evaluate the board of a well-known manufacturing company, which wanted to get the ball rolling on CEO succession planning. When we began our one-on-one reviews with board members, it became clear that relationships had badly broken down. The situation was so dire that some members weren't speaking to others, and cliques had formed, seriously skewing progress on people, skills and strategy.

Several individuals had developed acute emotional reactions to other personalities on the board and one person in particular was described (by several colleagues) with the words, "He just doesn't get it and isn't capable of operating at this level." There was obviously a movement towards ousting this person – stoked by private discussions on the topic. Yet this person was seen, by others, as a potential next CEO and a key player in the organisation's future. They described him as a skilled navigator, who could understand where the company needed to go to survive in a turbulent market.

Sadly, board meetings had become incredibly tense, brimming with unresolved questions about talent and strategy. People were advocating their views, prompting vigorous agreement from their own camp, and obvious frustration from the other camp (huffing, eye-rolling and so on). Board discussions on most topics had become mired in these personal differences, causing a severe knock-on effect on decision-making. In fact, constructive talk about any significant issues had become difficult, and reaching consensus was impossible. This meant that decisions were taken by block voting, leaving the minority feeling irritated and disillusioned. Even worse, problems were spiralling downwards in the organisation, with senior management taking sides in the tussle over future strategic direction.

As we continued our evaluation, board members began to contact us privately, pointing the finger of blame and lobbying for their own positions. Several openly suggested we recommend others should be replaced, as they "lacked the necessary skills."

At the time, we felt the weight of this emotionally charged situation and struggled to come up with easy answers. What could we do to help this board navigate such a fraught situation? During the years since this client scenario, we've learnt that there are no silver bullets, but that self-awareness, paying attention to relationships and making tactical interventions, can help people find a way through.

That's what this book is all about.

Acknowledgements

Our heartfelt thanks go to the 40 board interviewees who spent so much time and energy sharing the wisdom they amassed over years of working at board level in various sectors. Their openness in telling us about their experiences – good and bad – with a view to helping others navigate the labyrinth of board relationships, has made this book what it is. The consensus amongst them was that anonymity would enable them to speak more freely, so we won't name them individually, but they know who they are!

We are indebted to the coaches, board advisors and facilitators who kindly contributed their professional insights and practical advice, in particular Julie Allan, Laurence Barrett, Hannah Burd, Georgina Cavaliere, Lynne Chambers, Emma Chilvers, Clint Evans, Margaret Heffernan, Dr Sam Humphrey, Julie Jones, Jana Klimecki, Jonathan Males, Henry Marsden, Shauna McVeigh and Georgina Woudstra. We're also grateful to the board clients and colleagues we have worked with and learnt from over the years. They've helped us develop our own understanding of boardroom relationship dynamics, just as they've forged their own skills and style.

We appreciate our early readers who gave us feedback on initial drafts of this book and helped us hone the concepts, structure and content. We made vast improvements thanks to Barry Fletcher, Dr Keith Goodall, Professor John Hailey, Professor Emeritus Veronica Hope Hailey and William Winston. And we owe immense thanks to the reviewers of the final draft – who acted as our essential outside eyes: Ben Norman, Jane Molloy, Ian Roberts, Andrew Wood and Joy's colleagues at Praesta Partners LLP, namely Nick Brown, Pete Freeman, Janet Rubin and Peter Shaw. We'd particularly like to acknowledge the role that Claire Harcup, Stuart Hopper and Shauna McVeigh have played in producing this book. Despite busy lives, they were constant sources of support and guidance to us.

Our gratitude goes to those who helped with the hard yards of interview transcription and text editing, including Madi Hopper, Joanna Shaw, Pete Valente and Louise Smith. Louise, your expert editing and wicked humour made us laugh at ourselves – thank you. We salute the creative work of Andrew Wood and Michael Burdett on the appealing illustrations and sourcing the cover design respectively. Thanks also go to Routledge for their immediate faith in the book concept and the always prompt and helpful input of the editorial team.

Our families, friends and colleagues have been a great support to us during the book's gestation. We can't thank them enough for their encouragement, tolerance and many cups of tea. They include Joy's family, Hugh, Gemma and Ben, Mary and John, sister Claire and her partner Michael. And Helen's family, Stuart, Madi and Charlie, her h3 business partners and kindred spirits, Emma Chilvers, Hilary Duggan, Shauna McVeigh and Andrew Wood, and her colleagues and friends at The Listening Place. Also, to everyone who tactfully asked how the book was going and endured the response "We're nearly there!"

Neither of us could have written the book on our own; we each brought different perspectives, strengths, ideas and passionately held views. We also had fun working together – it was particularly entertaining to notice that, as deadlines loomed, we exhibited the kind of defensive behaviour we were writing about! In short, we appreciated each other's company as we made our way down a winding, fruitful path.

Finally, thanks to Leaders' Quest for first bringing the two of us together at an extraordinary retreat in India and – closer to home – to the perfect equidistant haunt: the Hawk Inn, Amport, a cosy and conducive place to mull over ideas and cook up a book.

Introduction

As a senior independent director, I would say 80% of my time was spent managing the emotional and relationship side – that was the task.
Former CEO, chair and non-executive director of FTSE 100 companies

Every board needs healthy relationships to function smoothly

As a board member, you tend to know when your board is working together well. There is mutual respect between members, who appreciate each other's differences and opinions. Discussion is open and animated and, when times are tough, you pull together to find a way forward. You trust that everyone has the organisation's best interests at heart. A survey of 640 chairs and non-executive directors from across the globe, by the London Business School and others [1], concludes that the quality of relationship "dynamics can make or break the success of the board." It confirms what most board members instinctively sense – their capacity to interact effectively with each other is essential to drive performance.

In contrast, "poor dynamics can paralyse a board as decisions get made and re-made." Crucial conversations happen offline, "rather than around the boardroom table, and status games silence some board members, which stifles innovation and diverse thinking." And yet upwards of a third of those surveyed mentioned there was no debate on their board, and a third said there was excessive personal conflict. This indicates that there is dysfunctional behaviour on a substantial percentage of boards.

In our research for this book, we interviewed executive and non-executive board members from a wide variety of sectors. They shared the view that effective working relationships make a board more responsive and agile. As one FTSE 100 director explains "*Good board dynamics allow a company to get after a problem faster*" rather than "*papering over the cracks*". In good times or bad, if a board's conducted well, it's a safe place to table and debate important issues. A CEO, for example, can discuss topics openly and receive support and challenge

DOI: 10.4324/9780429340239-1

that broadens their perspective. This sharpens thinking and allows swift and effective reactions to emerging opportunities and risks. And what happens at the top of an organisation tends to be reflected below, so the positive effects of collaborative relationships are likely to ripple through an organisation.

The clear message from our interviewees is that good dynamics elevate members' capacity to contribute, making the board so much more than the sum of its parts. They also agree that healthy relationships prevent a board being deflected away from strategy and towards dealing with personality clashes and power struggles. In short, boards can really get down to business when they tap into individual capabilities and focus on organisational strategy and performance. Yet despite this recognition of the value of healthy board dynamics, we heard many accounts of boards being diverted by interpersonal problems and struggling to solve them. Why is it challenging to address these difficulties? Because, in the words of one non-executive *"The emotional things are much more difficult to describe, much more difficult to manage."*

We believe that the capacity to use self-awareness to relate well to others and manage relationships will be an increasingly vital and differentiating skill for board members. We think that in addition to traditional education on setting direction, monitoring performance and managing risk, board members from school governors to multinational corporations need a kitbag of tactics to improve their relationships. This will enable boards to liberate themselves from difficult dynamics and focus their attention on the work at hand.

The purpose of this book

As executives, non-executives and advisors ourselves, we've spent decades working with boards, and we've discovered a wealth of invaluable ideas and techniques – driven by psychology – for improving interactions and relationships.

This book is a practical guide for people who want to understand how to manage difficult board dynamics and improve organisational performance. It's aimed at current board members, those who are equipping themselves to take on such leadership roles and their advisors and coaches.

We focus on human nature individually and in groups – rather than procedure and governance – and our insights are relevant across sectors, size or age of organisation and countries. Our principles are applicable to any areas where people work together to achieve a common goal.

Practical advice from experienced board members

In writing this book, we interviewed 40 experienced board members, who generously shared nuggets of practical advice, gleaned from years of trial and error.

Drawn from a range of cultural backgrounds and generations, most had held executive and non-executive positions; many had sat on a variety of boards. We spoke to members in the corporate, professional services, public and charity/social purpose sectors. The board members and advisors we interviewed typically worked with medium or large organisations, and many also had experience in smaller enterprises. Most were UK-based, but we were careful to include perspectives from a broad range of geographies, including the Global North and South. Many of our interviewees had portfolio board careers, encompassing corporate-through-to-social-enterprise roles. Others were at an earlier stage of their career, often encouraged by their employer to sit on not-for-profit boards or committees, to develop leadership skills for the future.

We conducted focus groups of board advisors, including executive coaches, and board development, evaluation and mediation specialists. This additional research helped us to identify common boardroom dynamics issues and figure out how to tackle them and foster a high-performing board.

We also drew on our own experiences, especially our most recent portfolio careers in executive coaching, executive and board evaluation and development, and a variety of executive and non-executive roles on boards. We incorporated learnings from our early work experiences – Joy as a lawyer specialising in commercial dispute resolution, and Helen as a management consultant for large scale transformation programmes.

Throughout this book, our interviewees will share their experiences, offer practical advice and act as "personal advisors" to you, the reader. They'll explain how they tackled difficult dynamics in their own boardrooms, and what they learnt on the way. Their stories and wise words are peppered through the topics, and you'll find their tried and tested tactics at the end of each chapter.

Psychological guides to difficult dynamics

Our research identified seven common types of difficult boardroom dynamic happening at main, subsidiary, and committee level. In the following chapters we explore each board challenge in turn:

- Balancing executive/non-executive seesaws – sharing power between different roles.
- Negotiating the standoff – finding a way ahead when your board is divided and has reached an impasse on an important issue.
- Banishing bullying – handling domineering or coercive behaviour.
- Activating the passive rubber stamp board – enabling it to assert its authority.
- Descending the ivory tower – becoming more in touch with your markets, your organisation, and its stakeholders.

- Harnessing diversity – making better decisions by drawing on a broad range of perspectives.
- Facing up to a doomsday scenario – pulling together when your board encounters a crisis that threatens its very existence.

Board members often point to personality clashes as the cause of relationship difficulties in these scenarios. Or they blame the presence of too many strong egos in the room. Yes, some board members may be egotistical – self-important and used to having their own way. And understanding your own personality, and appreciating the traits of others who are different, is an important part of developing a well-functioning board. But in our experience, factors like personality and ego are the tip of the iceberg, and there are usually other psychological elements underlying difficult dynamics.

The psychology of individual behaviour and group dynamics provides insights into what's going on beneath the surface of challenging board situations. So we've paired the seven relationship scenarios with the pertinent ideas of some key psychologists. As this is a diverse discipline, we've selected boardroom-relevant concepts from three distinct schools of psychology:

- Psychodynamics (working with hidden motives).
- Cognitive behavioural psychology (managing mindsets).
- Neuroscience (regulating your nervous system).

We've picked the most useful ideas and models from each school – those commonly used by us and the advisors and coaches we interviewed. In our experience, these concepts can help you to understand what's happening with relationships in the boardroom and why – and they offer helpful ideas about how to improve things.

We begin with psychodynamic theories that have stood the test of time since the early development of psychology in the 19th century. We continue through to 20th-century findings on cognitive behavioural psychology, and 21st-century research on neuroscience. You'll see that, rather than offering competing explanations of human behaviour, these theories provide complementary perspectives on the fundamentals of human relationships and interactions.

We've organised the book into three parts, each focusing on one of these three schools of psychology. We begin each part with a short introduction to the psychological theory, then we apply it to some of the boardroom scenarios outlined above (see Figure 0.1). For simplicity, we've applied one area of psychological theory to each particular scenario. But in practice you will usually find the psychology can be relevant in other situations (depending on what you find appealing and useful).

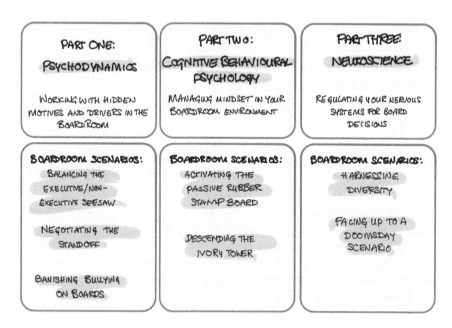

Figure 0.1 Schools of psychology and difficult dynamics

In our final chapter we combine insights from each of the approaches, and ask what they mean for boardroom relationships in the future.

Part One: Psychodynamics in the boardroom – Hidden motives and drivers

We begin by looking at boardroom relationships from a psychodynamic per-spective. Psychodynamic theories focus on the psychological drives and forces within you, and how these shape your behaviour, personality and experiences in groups. They often explore early childhood as a way of understanding what under-lies your thoughts and actions. This area of psychology takes a particular interest in the parts of your mind that are inaccessible – your unconscious feelings and motivations.

In Part One, we invite you to reflect on the potential impact of unconscious drivers – on individual relationships with your fellow board members, and on the culture of your whole group. First, we consider this in the context of the executive/non-executive seesaw, exploring how to manage this delicate balance of power. Next, we examine what could be happening unconsciously when your board is split on a fundamental issue, and you need to resolve a standoff. We then look at bullying and consider how to tackle overbearing or coercive boardroom behaviour.

Part Two: Cognitive behavioural psychology – Managing your mindset in the boardroom environment

In Part Two, we switch to a contrasting perspective – cognitive behavioural psychology. Psychologists working in this area pursue the scientific study of the cause-and-effect relationships between your environment and your behaviour, and the way in which your mindset shapes them (and is shaped by them). We examine how features of your boardroom environment might exacerbate or inhibit behaviour, and the role of your own thought processes in preventing or enabling change.

We apply these psychological concepts to the relationship between a board and its wider environment. We consider boards that are unable to exert their authority and find themselves rubber stamping decisions made elsewhere. Then we look at ivory tower boards – those which have lost touch with reality. We ask how these complacent boards can find out what is really going on in their organisations and the environments in which they operate.

Part Three: Neuroscience in the boardroom – How your brain and body's nervous system affect your behaviour

Part Three illuminates your boardroom relationships with insights from neuroscience. Psychologists in this speciality use techniques like brain imaging, and analysis of the chemical and electrical workings of our nervous systems, to explain our experiences and actions. We look at situations in which your brain and wider nervous system is wired to attract you to some people, and skew your decision-making in favour of the comfortably familiar. We ask how boards can harness diverse perspectives in pursuit of better decisions. Finally, we step into a doomsday scenario, in which the board faces an existential crisis. Here we learn about the make-or-break power of relationships when dealing with difficult choices and their consequences. We review the impact of extreme stress on your mind and body, and how this can manifest itself around your board table.

Advice: Acquiring the ART of boardroom dynamics

For each of our seven difficult boardroom dynamics, we present a selection of actionable advice, based on psychological theory and our research. These wise words represent the advice you would receive if you could consult expert psychologists or ask experienced board veterans directly for their counsel. Managing boardroom relationships is an art, and our advice for handling these situations has three main elements (see Figure 0.2):

- **Awareness**: when you're stuck in a difficult situation, it can be tempting to place the blame, and the responsibility for resolving it, onto others. But if they're uninterested in changing, things will stay the same – unless you alter something. So we present ways to build awareness of your own role in the situation. We help you recognise when you might be inadvertently contributing to an issue, or passively enabling it. And we offer ways of generating options for moving towards a resolution.
- **Relating**: once you're armed with awareness and options, you're ready to make conscious choices about how you relate to others. We share advice on improving your approach to relationships and altering your habits of interacting with board colleagues and other stakeholders, to create healthier dynamics.
- **Tactics**: it's helpful to build a toolkit of tactics from which you can select and deploy techniques to manage and resolve difficult dynamics. We pass on tried and tested tactics – for shifting the dynamic on your board – which have proved useful to our board interviewees and their advisors.

How to use this book

Each chapter has the following, easy-to-navigate features:

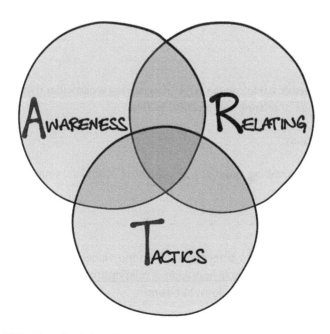

Figure 0.2 ART of board relationships

Introduction

We describe a common boardroom relationship challenge revealed from our research and give illustrations of this kind of complex boardroom situation.

What are you noticing?

We look at the typical symptoms, so you can get a feel for whether your board might be experiencing this kind of difficulty.

Inside story

We use a story, based on a combination of real situations from our research, to bring each challenging dynamic to life. These case studies are composites – we have changed specifics to protect anonymity. They equip you to recognise similar situations and allow you to work out how you might respond.

Psychological roots

We use psychological theory to illuminate the underlying causes of the problem and point the way towards resolving it. Understanding these roots can help build awareness of yourself and others, and allow you to make conscious choices about how best to resolve problems.

Advice

We offer actionable advice on the ART of mastering a particular dynamic through awareness, ways of relating and practical tactics.

Crucial questions

These thought-provoking questions are useful to stimulate your thinking about your specific situation.

Power tools

These are effective models or methods – from individual and group development specialists. You can use them to help address relationship dynamics, unlock change and liberate your board to get down to business.

Summary

A brief reminder of the themes covered in the chapter.

Further reading

A short reading list for further exploration.

One last thing ...

Before we get started, it's worth reiterating that it's a lifelong journey to understand yourself and an elusive quest to truly understand other people. Whilst it's tempting to use psychological concepts to diagnose or label people and relationships, this misunderstands their usefulness. In these pages, we present our chosen psychological concepts as prompts to self-reflection – spurs to curiosity about your own role in an unfolding situation. We urge you to hold the concepts lightly and try to stimulate your own self-awareness (rather than deciding that your colleague is in the grip of an unconscious narcissistic impulse)! Ask yourself why you might be responding in a particular way, own the part you play in a difficult boardroom situation and consider what you can do to improve it. At times it can be hard to answer these questions on your own, so we suggest enlisting the support of colleagues, a critical friend or an executive coach as a sounding board for this fundamental enquiry.

We hope you will read this book from cover to cover, but you can also use it to go straight to a tricky boardroom dynamic you may be experiencing. Or you can head straight to our advice sections (towards the end of each chapter), which work as stand-alone reads. Whatever your approach, we hope it will become a well-thumbed companion throughout your board career, and a personal mentor that helps you foster clarity and collaboration in times of tension.

Part One

Psychodynamics

Hidden motives and drivers

Psychological painkillers

From the psychodynamic viewpoint, much of the dysfunctional behaviour of individuals or groups is driven by unconscious responses to the anxiety felt in relationships. To cope with anxiety, we develop defence mechanisms – unconscious means of protecting ourselves (knowingly or unknowingly) against emotional discomfort and pain. These defensive manoeuvres range from the simple act of choosing to delay a difficult conversation, to a board's unspoken agreement to ignore basic differences of opinion on a matter of strategic importance. The leadership scholar and psychoanalyst Manfred Kets de Vries [2] characterises these defensive moves as psychological painkillers – self-prescribed protection from anxiety and emotional pain.

At one level, as with regular painkillers, this can be quite functional. Defences enable us to manage pain within tolerable bounds so that we can continue to operate effectively. However, continued reliance can have unwanted side-effects. It also treats the symptoms alone, whereas it's useful, at some point, to turn our attention to the underlying causes. For example, simply becoming aware that we sometimes act defensively (to unconsciously protect ourselves) opens the possibility of making more conscious choices about our actions. We can then change the impact we have on people around us, which in turn alters their responses. Furthermore, tuning into the ways in which emotional dynamics emerge (just from the experience of being in a group), enables us – as board members – to work with these psychological forces. It becomes possible to manage them, instead of finding ourselves at their mercy.

Psychodynamic greats

In the following three chapters, we look at the ideas of Sigmund Freud, the father of psychodynamic thinking, and others who have built on his ideas, including his daughter Anna Freud, and Melanie Klein. We also draw on the work of three later

DOI: 10.4324/9780429340239-2

luminaries in the psychodynamic tradition, who took a particular interest in groups: Wilfred Bion, Eric Berne and Elliott Jaques. Research and experience suggest their theories are highly relevant when it comes to forging effective board relationships.

Applying their ideas and insights to the boardroom, we analyse three difficult dynamics. First, we examine what might be going on – unconsciously – when executives and non-executives jointly hold power on a board. We consider situations where this finely balanced relationship moves from collegiate collaboration to power struggle, and suggest ways to balance on this seesaw of constantly shifting power. Next, we visit boardrooms where positions have hardened, and different sides and factions are deadlocked in a standoff situation. Here we explore the possible psychodynamic roots of these relationship breakdowns and consider what might be done to find a way forward together. Finally, we turn to the topic of bullying on boards, and focus on the perspective of the bystander. We address what happens, subliminally, when board colleagues fail to intervene and how this can be overcome. For each of these situations, we tap into boardroom veterans' experience to gain practical advice on easing these difficulties.

From curiosity to self-awareness

It's impossible to know, definitively, the nature of a psychodynamic force, despite seeing, feeling and sometimes even predicting its effects. Highly skilled therapists can only hazard informed hypotheses about what's happening unconsciously within another person or a group and proceed on that basis. For this reason, as we mentioned in the introduction, we recommend you use the psychodynamic concepts that follow simply to fuel your curiosity and empathy. As prompts to reflect, rather than ways to pigeon-hole or diagnose people. They are undoubtedly a useful way to stimulate your own emotional self-awareness (and that of your board) and ask yourself how your relationships might become healthier.

Chapter 1

Balancing executive/non-executive seesaws

I think there will always be a tension and most executives will, at one stage or another, believe that the non-executives are interfering. The good ones will push back with common sense as to where management stops and governance begins. The ones that aren't so good find it difficult to find that boundary.

Senior independent director, international financial services firm

Introduction

The chair of a fast-moving consumer goods (FMCG) enterprise shared an experience of working with a successful CEO who was operating increasingly independently of his board of directors. The business had been moving towards a more environmentally sustainable business model for some time, with this high-profile CEO as the public face of its endeavour. He had been recruited by the company because of his passion for sustainability and radical ideas about its future. But more and more often, he and his executive team were stating their intentions about next steps, without agreeing a direction with the board. Some of these next steps required significant long-term investment in infrastructure, and over several meetings, non-executive directors on the board began to voice their financial concerns. They pushed for a strategic review by the whole board, but gained lukewarm support from the CEO.

Once the board had managed to agree a robust long-term investment strategy, the non-executives began to query the CEO's ability to deliver it. A scientist by training, he had spent much of his career in product development, with several genuinely ground-breaking designs to his name. But when he applied his creativity to the organisation's supply chain and production methods, the board feared he lacked the commercial acumen to ensure financial viability. In return, the CEO accused the directors of being bean counters who just wanted to maintain the status quo and extract more money. Detailed financial plans were sparse, so it was hard for the board to monitor progress as the CEO's transformation plans gathered pace. As the non-executives became increasingly uncomfortable, they began to press for

DOI: 10.4324/9780429340239-3

more information, saying "*We have expectations about the reports that we receive, and these reports are inadequate.*" The CEO and his team were feeling increasingly frustrated that their board colleagues could not see beyond the immediate financials, and appreciate their vision of transforming the sector.

This kind of struggle is common, because being a board member presents a significant challenge. It's a high-pressure environment, which requires a group to hold power together. This is particularly tricky to do when legal responsibility for the organisation is jointly held between executive and non-executive roles on a unitary board, as is common in Australia, Singapore, South Africa, the UK, Spain and the USA. On these boards, there is usually a clear delineation of roles, with executives accountable for day-to-day running of the organisation, and non-executive directors taking a more detached oversight role, especially in areas of strategy and risk. Plus, there's a hierarchy, with a chair at the helm and a CEO leading the organisation. There are sometimes designated elder roles, like senior independent director in the UK, and lead director or presiding director in the USA. Despite this structure, no single role commands ultimate control, and this means power can shift between individuals and groups on a board. This produces the executive/non-executive seesaw: the delicate balance of power between two groups.

These turf wars betray an underlying tension: who is actually calling the shots? There is no simple answer to this question, which means that, in addition to their explicit tasks, people on boards must continually work to find and maintain a mutual balance of power. As one public sector chair puts it, to maintain equilibrium on the seesaw of power, constant effort is required by non-executives to find and walk "*the tiny line of being too much or too little involved.*" It requires close attention to the subtle signals indicating where influence is held, how it is being used and to what ends. Is it being used to satisfy individuals or groups? Or for the good of the organisation and its stakeholders? Or perhaps to serve broader purposes? It also means finding practical ways to rebalance executive and non-executive authority within a board.

In this chapter we review the early warning signs that executives and non-executives are venturing into each other's territory and causing frustration. To illustrate these signs, we examine an inside story of non-executive overreach on a FTSE 100 board, and explore the psychological roots of these issues. We consider the unconscious motivations that might lie behind these uses and abuses of power, and look at practical steps taken by board members to restore a healthy balance of power.

What are you noticing? The power seesaw

How can you spot emerging difficulties in maintaining a functional balance of power within your board? The board members and coaches we interviewed mentioned various signs of potential trouble.

Muscling in

Several of the stories told to us involved non-executives struggling to sit on their hands. Often driven by a well-intentioned desire to contribute, and lacking an alternative playbook, they tended to fall back on a blueprint from early in their executive careers. The ensuing stumble into executive territory can be unsettling or irritating for executives at best, and interpreted as an act of disrespect or aggression at worst. One chair of a charity described a situation where a non-executive was *"On a matter of some importance, delving and diving in lower down the organisation. Saying 'it shall be so', without even telling the CEO, let alone clearing their lines of authority in advance."* In his view, the non-executive's actions were ill-advised, and compounded by their failure to acknowledge this incursion and offer the CEO a genuine apology for the disruption caused.

Another CEO described competing executive and non-executive power bases on the board of a private equity-backed business.

> *You've got a chair who wants to be listened to because they're an investor ... You've got the non-executive founder who thinks they know because they started the business. And you've got the CEO who believes they have the answer because they're running the business.*

It was ultimately very frustrating for this CEO, coping with different voices who each thought they had the most relevant knowledge. She was *"constantly educating people ... trying to get everybody into a common understanding of where we are as a business"* and their respective roles in building for the future.

Shutting out

As we've shown in the FMCG scenario at the beginning of this chapter, CEOs sometimes shut out other directors or trustees to regain or retain power. In an ideal situation, board colleagues see each other as allies, and feel able to draw on each other's perspectives, expertise, knowledge and insights. It's dangerous when executives on boards shut themselves off from this valuable resource, due to insecurity, excessive confidence, personality traits or sometimes a heady mixture of all three. As an expert chair summarised,

> *I've seen CEOs who see the board as the enemy and are thinking how they can keep them off their back. Good CEOs are open with – "here's what's going well, here's what I'm struggling with, and this is what I need help with."*

A board member of one public sector organisation described the following situation: *"The CEO just felt that the chair was too much on his territory and couldn't see that if he satisfied the chair, it was an advantage, as opposed to fighting him."* This CEO withheld information from the board and, in discussions, went straight to *"Just keep off my territory."* Ideally, he'd have started from the position that the chair's views ought to be considered, because they are probably sensible and reasonable.

Paying lip service

When collective responsibility breaks down between executives and non-executives, it can be a sign that seesaw dynamics are emerging. Perhaps the CEO agrees to a board-suggested downsizing strategy, but in practice takes no action to reduce the cost-base. Often one side or the other resorts to saying *"Yes"* simply to appear co-operative, but they fail to follow through on their agreement. Their actions do not mirror their words.

One non-executive of a national utility company shared the example of a colleague who he felt had a severe case of over-confidence, bordering on hubris. *"He was all powerful and it completely affected the whole business structure. I think there's a genuine danger in business that if an individual is too successful, it goes to their head."* This colleague would play along in board conversations, but afterwards act as though the discussion had never happened. He would go his own way, and if colleagues queried this, he'd brief them to follow him. The non-executive was alarmed by this show of arrogance because of his belief that *"Business is too complicated to know it all."*

Questioning competence

When pressure builds and trust wanes, executives and non-executives often begin to question each other's actions, performance and (eventually) competence to hold their roles. Serious challenges to individual positions inevitably destabilise the board's balance of power. People jockey for positions and retaliate with challenges of their own. As we saw in the FMCG story at the start of this chapter, groups of executives or non-executives can come together to question the legitimacy of a colleague on the other side of a divide. At one level, this questioning is a healthy part of board functioning – no one member is above the collective judgement of their peers. But a board on which executives and non-executives are intent on undermining each other is inevitably going to sabotage its own performance. Table 1.1 summarises the classic symptoms of a tussle between executive and non-executive power.

Table 1.1 What are you noticing? The power seesaw

Over-reach	Board members persistently operate beyond their remit, without the consent of their colleagues.
Avoidance	Executives avoid informal contact with their non-executive colleagues, and seek to minimise discussion of important topics.
Broken commitments	Individual members fail to take collective responsibility for positions and fail to follow through on decisions reached at the board.
Role challenges	Board members seriously question the competence of one or more of their fellow members to hold their role.

The following inside story explores how this type of power struggle can play out in practice.

Inside story: Non-executive over-reach

A non-executive of a FTSE 100 company described a salutary experience to us. He had recently secured two non-executive chair positions of well-performing companies, and was feeling pleased that his long aspired-to portfolio career was coming along nicely. However, within six months of taking up these positions, both CEOs came to him (independently) saying *"People have been asking whether you're an executive or non-executive."* In his own mind he'd been striving to add value quickly, but now saw that both CEOs were questioning his well-intentioned efforts. He knew they were issuing him with a diplomatically worded warning to back off. This feedback was disquieting the first time, and deeply concerning the second. It stopped him in his tracks and prompted some deep self-reflection.

This chair had the courage and curiosity to approach his other board colleagues and ask for feedback on his first six months of chairing. Some common themes emerged. One observed that his digital transformation expertise meant he was contributing in some depth to this topic during management presentations from non-board members. This colleague noted that, at times, management really liked his interjections because of the constructive challenge and learning. *"They were quite excited by the level of engagement and dialogue. But the executive and the non-executives often also felt that it was too intrusive – he'd crossed the Rubicon."*

Another reflected that, under his chairing, board meetings quickly deteriorated into *"operational solutionising"*, which would be better done by managers in the business. In short, they found that whilst the chair was clearly a great CEO, the board already had an excellent CEO, and this overlap was problematic. A colleague explained,

> *When you default to your comfort zone of CEO by asking me for details about the status of projects, I start to bring things to you as if you are holding that role. And it becomes a very confusing, vicious circle.*

Overall, executives were generally surprised at the level and frequency of communication the chair was having with them. And they were concerned by the extent of his presence within the wider business. He seemed to be popping up here, there and everywhere. Asking questions, delving into details and checking up on things. This was disruptive for staff who felt uncomfortable under the gaze of such a senior figure, and it had his executive colleagues wondering what he was up to, and why. One pointed out that his reach into the business had another unfortunate consequence in board discussions: his micro-interactions across the organisation meant he gained current, local insights, which he was not shy to use to shut down executive colleagues' arguments.

Thinking back over this feedback and his non-executive roles, the chair reflected that all of them, to a greater or lesser extent, have been frustrating. He explained "*I'm by nature a command and control, old school operational manager.*" Although he hoped that he listened well, he did like the challenge of "*Doing stuff rather than sitting back, contemplating, and just advising. Which to some extent is the role of a non-executive.*" When he saw businesses doing things which, from a commercial perspective, he thought they shouldn't, he wanted to intervene. His natural reaction was to "*Bang the table, metaphorically speaking, and say, 'Don't do that, it's silly, do this instead.'*" In his head he knew this wouldn't work, and it's not the chair's role to tell the executive what to do. But in the moment, it was hard to resist.

On one level his diligence was impressive, but it was fuelling deep mistrust between the chair and the executive team. The chair could see the writing on the wall. He needed to step back to give the executive space to operate. He knew trust was important, and yet he could see significant problems ahead for one of the two businesses. The organisation was going full throttle on simultaneous transformation across multiple territories and services. From his executive experience in a similar market, he was certain these were foolhardy tactics. Sitting on his hands as chair, he felt the frustration of being powerless to stop his naive board stumbling into real peril.

We'll return to this story to see how this was resolved, but first let's examine the psychological roots of similar situations.

Psychological roots: From defensive moves to self-awareness

We've seen that power sharing can lead to tension between non-executives and executives. From a psychodynamic perspective, the source and impact of each party's power has several aspects. Power can be partly external, coming from the status and role that the organisation or wider environment endows on us, as board members. Its source is also internal, emanating from our beliefs, drives and motivations to succeed. The management of this power happens through our relationships with others – how we position ourselves in relation to them. As Anton Obholzer neatly puts it in the revealing book *The Unconscious at Work,* sharing power "requires recognition of where one's role ends and another person's begins, the scope and limits of one's own authority and a readiness to sanction that of others" [3].

So how do we personally react, within ourselves, to power sharing across sometimes blurred boundaries? Do we embrace it and have the confidence and ability to deliver what is needed? Or does it cause us to fret? We're likely to find situational factors have a profound influence on these feelings towards others. For instance, a CEO might be perfectly calm about non-executives inquiring into their operational domain when things are going well, but may become anxious and hold their cards close to their chest when the organisation is starting to fail. It's the acceptance of other people's authority, and the emotions this evokes, that is often most difficult for board members. As Obholzer observes "Rivalry, jealousy and envy often interfere with the process of taking up either a leadership or followership role" [3]. It's the competitiveness that can come from being close to power, and endeavouring to share it, that we see as particularly problematic on executive/non-executive boards.

According to psychodynamic theory, the psychological pain of feelings of insecurity, distrust and even inadequacy can trigger us to act unknowingly to protect ourselves from this discomfort. We act in unconscious, irrational ways to defend against perceived threats to our identity and our sense of who we are. In studying defences like these, Sigmund Freud developed the set of psychological theories and therapeutic techniques known as psychoanalysis. Through these, he sought to explore how our unconscious mind operates to minimise the pain we feel. Freud used the term *defence mechanisms* to describe the mental processes by which this happens, and developed theories about their predictable workings.

Psychological defence mechanisms

Through painstaking analysis of patients in his consulting room, Freud mapped out a revolutionary theory of personality [4]. He described the human mind as comprising separate elements. Whilst we are aware of some parts (the conscious), others are hidden from view (the unconscious). This opens up the possibility that different parts of a person's mind can interact with each other – sometimes in ways they are unaware of. We might be able to hide our own thoughts, feelings and beliefs from ourselves, and be oblivious to the impact they nonetheless have on our own actions and relationships.

Freud identified a variety of mental moves employed by people as psychological defence mechanisms. Ways of protecting beliefs about ourselves, which we find reassuring, from being challenged by others, or by situations we're part of. His daughter Anna Freud [5] built on his ideas, elaborating on a set of core defence mechanisms. At the root is *repression* – the exclusion of feelings and wishes from our conscious awareness, to reduce anxiety. Hiding the pain. It's worth noting that, whilst the Freuds worked with patients suffering mental health problems, they saw these as extreme manifestations of mechanisms that are at work every day, in all of us. Their ideas have been adopted and adapted, and are still in extensive use by psychologists. Here, we focus on two defence mechanisms commonly used to repress fears and insecurities: *projection* and *transference*. Our practice and research suggest that these are particularly relevant to boardroom relationships.

Projecting feelings onto others

Projection is a psychological defence mechanism which involves avoiding emotions, by attributing our own unwanted thoughts, feelings and motives to another person. It's as if the other person is a screen onto which we can project our unacceptable thoughts and feelings. We can see and experience them, but from a safe distance, and separate from ourselves. For instance, because of a fear of failure in a new CEO role, we might feel a need to keep tight control of things and avoid sharing any details of problems or risks. Part of us might feel this impulse is unacceptable and unethical, so we resolve this conflict by believing that the chair and non-executives want to control us (and are in fact undermining us). We conclude that they are keeping us in the dark about important things.

What might our inside story chair be projecting when he over-reaches his remit? He's new to being a chair and wants to contribute well to this new chapter of his successful career. He knows it requires him to operate in new ways, but it's not clear to him what these might be. Perhaps he is anxious to protect his image of himself as successful. Perhaps he fears he is fundamentally incapable of meeting his colleagues' expectations. It's certainly interesting that he views them as naïve, and struggles to trust them to do a decent job, despite both companies having performed well with these people at the helm (long before his arrival). Could his discomfort with his own feelings of inadequacy lead him to project them onto his board colleagues? Perhaps this explains why he's acting as if they can't be trusted to meet his expectations. Perhaps it represents the real reason he feels the need to take a command-and-control style to avoid poor performance.

Transferring past relationships onto current ones

Freud [6] also identified another defence mechanism, called *transference* (similar to projection). This mechanism involves transferring feelings and attitudes towards a significant person – from your past life – onto a present-day person. The significant past-life person is often a parent or family member, and the powerful feelings may come from unresolved conflicts in that early relationship. Transference is most likely to happen in stressful situations, where there is some similarity between the present and the past, which triggers the association. For example, if you were extremely competitive with an older sibling when you were young, you might find yourself with an unconscious desire to compete with a board colleague who has a similar way of talking down to you.

Again, it may seem surprising that, unconsciously, we might treat one person as if they were someone else. Leadership coach Jonathan Males gives us a down-to-earth explanation: "*Your parents are your first leaders, and your siblings (or absence of them) are your first team – this is where you learn about these relationships.*" Implicitly and in unspoken ways, we absorb lessons about the rules of engagement. We find ways of being that are most likely to get the responses we're after and avoid unpleasant reactions from people close to us. And when a colleague strikes a chord with an early experience of being personally familiar with someone, we may find the subsequent interaction slipping into the grooves of that former close relationship.

What might our chair, who is over-extending himself, be transferring? The chair had been brought up in a fairly chaotic home, where both parents experienced physical and mental health issues. At times they struggled to manage day-to-day household activities, and money was scarce. He had learnt that he could not rely on his parents, and if things went wrong, they were unlikely to be able to fix them. As a child this was frightening for him, but he knew his parents were doing their best. They just didn't have it in them to do any better. So from a young age, if he saw problems brewing, he would take charge, roll up his sleeves and draw on his considerable ingenuity and resourcefulness to find solutions.

This self-reliance and initiative had propelled his career, but was now making it hard for him to let go and depend on his colleagues to deliver. Especially in situations where he could see things going wrong, he was transferring assumptions and feelings – about his mother and father – onto his executive colleagues. Feeling fearful they could not cope, he was stepping in to take charge and prevent impending disaster (rather than seeing his colleagues as capable people who could meet their responsibilities).

We can see that individual psychological defences like projection and transference might cause board members to challenge each other's competence and push at role boundaries. And that these defences are triggered by the experience of trying to collaborate with others in situations where there's a lot at stake. But what about the nature of the work itself, and how it is structured? How might that exacerbate seesaw dynamics in the boardroom?

Appropriate levels of work

Elliott Jaques, Canadian psychoanalyst-turned-management consultant, introduced the concept of social defence mechanisms in organisations. He explored how the arrangement of work and the workplace can evoke the unconscious defences of people working within them. In his pertinent book *The Requisite Organisation,* Jaques points out the perils of organisational structures and processes which are likely to activate deep-seated feelings of paranoia. Ones which tend to stir mutual suspicion and mistrust in people, breeding selfishness and unhealthy competition [7]. The executive/non-executive set up of boards can be seen as just such a structure. One where careful management is needed to prevent ambiguity about power and control from causing defensive reactions and tense relationships.

How can a board minimise the impact of structural pressures on its members? Jaques outlined a powerful model for organising enterprises around levels of work called *Stratified Systems Theory.* It's a framework for ensuring work is done at the appropriate level for people to contribute fully, and organisations to flourish [7]. He defined seven potential strata within organisations, using criteria like the complexity of the work, and how far ahead people are looking for the outcome of their actions and decisions. The board advisors we interviewed also recommended creating some clarity about the level of work required, which will vary from board to board. And they stressed the importance of asking searching questions about individual capability and willingness to operate at this level. This is because clarity over "*what's mine to do and what belongs to others*" creates useful boundaries between roles. It promotes focus and can reduce individual anxiety about what should be happening.

Building on the work of Jaques and his long-term colleague Gillian Stamp [8], coach and leadership advisor Laurence Barrett offers a simple model for clarifying levels of work. You can use his framework (Table 1.2) to clarify the level of work that the board needs to do, and gauge where it is currently operating. The model describes levels in businesses which sell products, but it can be adapted and applied to service-based, public sector or social enterprises. It's a useful exercise for your board to describe the work levels in terms specific to your own organisation, to really get a sense of how it applies to you.

In our inside story, the chair was finding himself drawn to Level Three – execution of strategy – which in his case related to the pace of a digital transformation programme. In some organisations this might be an appropriate topic for the board. But due to the size and maturity of this business, the CEO saw these rollout tactics as landing squarely in the executive realm. Perhaps the chair had what leadership specialist Georgina Cavaliere describes as an "*operator mindset.*" Such leaders "*are operating through the lens of their own personal experience ... They're still relying on their own resourcefulness and capability to get stuff done.*" Instead, they should be drawing on the resources of people around them and working through others to achieve the best outcome.

Whether it's a non-executive dipping down into a level of work more suited to the executive team, or executives struggling to rise to a level of work required by

Table 1.2 Levels of work

Level Six: Shape the industry.

How do you influence your industry? What are the prevailing social trends and patterns? How can you impact and shape these trends? What kinds of organisation will thrive in a future world?

Level Five: Position the organisation.

How do you stay ahead of your competitors? What business are you in? What are the sources of your competitive advantage? How do you influence the dynamics or structure of your marketplace?

Level Four: Shape strategy.

What products do you take to market and how? What products are needed over the next five years? What changes are necessary to build the right business system?

Level Three: Develop organisational systems.

How do you manage your organisation effectively and efficiently? What products do you sell? What systems do you use to purchase, distribute and sell these products? How do you ensure you meet your regulatory obligations?

Level Two: Manage processes.

How do you make sure the processes are followed thoroughly? What are the steps of the process and how do they link together?

Level One: Deliver simple tasks.

What do you do now? Do you know what step to take next? Was what you did right or wrong?

(Barrett, adapted from Jaques and Stamp [7, 8])

a board, this structural problem is likely to create friction. Jaques points out that it becomes very difficult to do the work that's required if the level above or below you is not operating well [7]. For example, what happens if the Level Five work (determining the vision and purpose of the organisation) is not done by a board? It becomes hard for executives to do the Level Four work (identifying the optimum strategies for change). And if too many people are crowded around a particular level of work, the system becomes inefficient. Plus, they are likely to start bumping up against one another. This can trigger defensive reactions, and these hamper an individual's ability to operate in a more mature and sophisticated way.

Functioning at inappropriate levels of work can happen because of capability constraints. In our inside story, the board chair was gravitating towards executive tasks because he felt comfortable and competent in this area. Perhaps he didn't yet have the capacity to operate at non-executive level, or wasn't well suited, in terms of personality and motivation, to do this type of work. Maybe he was also feeling pulled towards a real void of skills, energy or appetite amongst his executive colleagues.

One board advisor points out that it's difficult when someone doesn't seem capable of working at the level required by their board. "*You're asking something of someone who in a way isn't wired to do it.*" They may simply, at this point in their career, lack the experience and maturity to operate in that way, and there will be some people who never develop this capability. It can be hard to make calls about which levels of work are optimal for a particular board, and how individual members' capabilities match these levels. For this reason, it can help to bring in external expertise, perhaps as part of a board evaluation process, as we discuss later in this chapter's *Advice* section.

Inside story: What happened next?

Returning to developments in our inside story, the conversations that this chair had with his colleagues were illuminating. Catching his own strong reactions to their feedback, he took some time to mull it over. At first he reflected by himself, and then with a good friend and board veteran who had become a kind of mentor to him. Together they sorted through the feedback, the relationships and the feelings that had emerged from his past, and analysed the commercial realities of the situation.

It turned out that the mentor had received similar feedback on maintaining healthy boundaries in her own initial board appointments. Looking ahead to the end of his term, she counselled the chair to use the feedback evidence to review the type of leader this board needed to enable the organisation to thrive. With that in mind, he considered moving to work in a smaller family business that was seeking an executive style chair. But ultimately he decided to stay, and with the support of his mentor and a therapist, address the feelings of inadequacy he had been projecting onto his colleagues. This work on his defences and anxiety helped him to become better able to let go and empower others, whilst building confidence in his own capacity to operate in new environments and tolerate risk.

We've seen that the seesaw of power can lead to difficult psychological board dynamics. Now we consider what can be done to enable change in similar situations. What is the advice of our board members and coaches on the ART of balancing this seesaw, so that members can collaborate and work together flexibly?

Advice on balancing the executive/non-executive seesaw

Awareness: Exploring your own contribution

The first step in managing a difficult boardroom dynamic is to ask yourself some tough questions about your own contribution to it. But from deep within the eye of an emerging storm, it's remarkably hard to gain perspective. A CEO describes the challenge. When everyone around you says *"You're doing a brilliant job,"* it's tempting to bring in people who offer that kind of praise. *"That's dangerous because you need to know your weaknesses too. You need to gain a view of your whole self as a leader."* Ideally, this self-knowledge is developed over a lifetime of appraisals and feedback, pointing out your strengths and weaknesses. The reality is that many board members haven't been given this kind of developmental information along the way. So it makes sense to actively seek feedback – from board colleagues and your advisors – about the part you are playing in an emerging situation.

Board advisors and coaches often use psychometric profiling of personality and motivations as a stimulus for self-reflection, and to prompt insights. Research on personality since the 1980s converges on five main traits, or ways in which we differ from each other [9]. Easily remembered using the mnemonic OCEAN, they are:

- Openness: how open you are to ideas, experiences, and ways of doing things.
- Conscientiousness: how much you strive for achievement, see duties as important, exert self-discipline, and deliberate over matters.
- Extraversion: how warm, gregarious, positive and assertive you are and how much you seek activity and excitement.
- Agreeableness: how trusting, straightforward, modest, altruistic and sympathetic you are in your dealings with others.
- Neuroticism: how prone you are to feelings of anxiety, angry hostility to others, depression, self-consciousness, impulsivity and vulnerability.

There are several psychometric tools which elaborate on this basic model. Completing one, working through your own profile, then comparing it with your board colleagues to understand similarities and differences, can go some way to raising your mutual awareness and understanding. However, as we've already said, some of our beliefs, feelings and motivations are unconscious – and therefore invisible to us. We suggest going one step further and using the psychodynamic concepts like projection and transference (described in the *Psychological roots* section above) to surface these. This makes it easier to become aware of times when you project your present feelings onto others, or transfer emotions from your past relationships onto current colleagues.

On first sight, the idea of projection might seem strange. Is it really possible to deceive yourself by believing that your own uncomfortable feelings are possessed by others, rather than you? The best way to identify projection in yourself is to see whether you can catch yourself in the act. When you find yourself experiencing a strong emotional reaction to a board colleague, particularly when you feel a moral judgement rising up, pause to reflect. With your hand on your heart, is there any part of that judgement that you could level at yourself? This might be a difficult piece of enquiry, as your unconscious may be working hard to keep the uncomfortable reality at bay.

Transference can often be a complicated phenomenon, but you can ask yourself some simple questions to notice its effects on your relationships. After an emotionally charged exchange with a board colleague, it's worth considering the nature of your feelings and reflecting on their similarity to feelings you've experienced in previous relationships. Perhaps you feel controlled, ignored or angry, and can sketch links to early experiences of comparable feelings. However, transference can be positive too, so it's also worth watching out for feelings like excitement, intimacy or light-heartedness. These may be echoes of past connections, as much as features of your current relationship. In *Chapter 3: Banishing bullying*, we explore further the effect of childhood experiences on your reaction to present-day situations.

As well as this kind of self-reflection, it's also helpful to call on the support of a suitably skilled colleague, friend, mentor, coach or therapist as a companion on this voyage of self-discovery. There are many useful books you can use to explore this topic. We recommend Joseph Burgo's book, *Why Do I Do That?* [10] as an accessible guide to a wide range of defence mechanisms, and ways to discover how they might be operating in your day-to-day experiences and interactions.

Making time for self-reflection is key. Consider it an investment in time to think beyond decisions and actions, focus on what's motivating and driving your behaviour in the boardroom and examine how functional it is. As a retired executive confessed: "*It's a big regret in my career that I didn't allow myself to take the odd half day a month to clear the decks and just think.*" One non-executive on the board of a business she founded uncovered insights about her behaviour by creating space to reflect,

> *I'm constantly worried that changes in strategy are going to burn the business down. I know I annoy colleagues by saying: "Oh we've done that already, it didn't work." But if I can't bring that experience, I feel completely pointless – and ask, what am I doing here then?*

Brought up by parents who were both quite self-centred and controlling, and as a middle child of five, this woman had struggled to be heard during her early years. She realised she was transferring her feelings of frustration – towards her parents – onto board colleagues when she felt they weren't listening. Simply acknowledging this issue to herself and others helped ease this tension. By becoming more conscious of her feeling that she needed to be heard, she was better able to question, in the moment, whether she was over-reacting in certain situations. This enabled her to build more trust in the executive, and share power and responsibility with them more appropriately.

Crucial questions – Awareness

- Have my psychological defences been triggered?
- What is the impact on me and on others?

Relating: Forging and maintaining alignment

In addition to self-awareness, we've seen that well-defined boundaries are a vital ingredient of successful, collaborative executive and non-executive power sharing. They involve making sure that people are clear about roles and the level of work required – so that everyone has transparent mutual expectations about the nature and extent of their involvement. As Jaques advises, having explicit conversations to surface differing assumptions about roles, and working through any mismatches of expectations, can significantly reduce the likelihood of unconscious defensiveness.

Initial alignment

In our research, we discovered that boards experiencing difficult relationship dynamics often regret missed opportunities to invest more time in this earlier. There's a proverb that says "The best time to plant a tree was 20 years ago. The second-best time is now." The same principle applies to forging mutual understanding of roles and boundaries. One classic way of achieving this is through facilitated discussion, led by an external board development specialist. The facilitator can convene and manage a series of board interactions specifically designed to strengthen relationships.

One CTO in digital financial services described such an experience. His facilitator worked individually with each of his fellow board members to create clarity around personality, motivations, expertise and capacity to contribute. Then she gathered them together to explore a series of questions, asking

> *You've got the executive team, the board, sub-committees – what are the key responsibilities and qualities of each? Given your roles, your experiences, how will each of you contribute? And how do you want to be accountable to each other for those things?*

What the executive found interesting about everyone's responses was how distinct people's opinions of their responsibilities were, and *"How they differed from the actual formal definition."* This was compounded by a mismatch between intentions and the reality of actual execution. In this case, all the board members loved the fact that it was their official responsibility to set the strategy. But when it came to it, from a practical point of view, they could not commit sufficient time together to actually develop the strategy. They quickly accepted it was impractical, and they needed the executive team to run the process on their behalf, with agreed ground rules. Plus a mechanism for the non-executives, in particular, *"to have a view into it, with enough levers to have influence"* on the final strategy.

Staying aligned

It's very powerful to use this kind of exercise to establish roles and responsibilities when a new board is formed, or there's a significant turnover of members. But there is also the ongoing work of ensuring members maintain this alignment in their roles and positions. This work is two-fold. Circling back around agreements made on roles and boundaries, to hold each other accountable, and stepping back to ask whether those roles and boundaries are still appropriate. Many of our interviewees pointed out the importance of finding ways to check in on agreements, find out how they are working in practice, and manage areas where there is unhelpful friction. They described this happening in a variety of ways: from being a formal part of board business or a board evaluation process, to carefully judged informal conversations. Some non-executives, particularly chairs, vice chairs and those in senior independent and lead director roles, found themselves drawn to this vital work.

Ideally, these changes in roles and boundaries happen gradually and consciously, through negotiation, and to suit the circumstances. For example, non-executives new to an organisation may have a legitimate need to delve into the operational realm to gain sufficient understanding of the enterprise. Afterwards, they will draw back to a position of oversight, more aligned with their non-executive role. Also, experienced or long-standing executives may hold significant power on the board, arising from the strength and depth of their connection with the organisation. Over time, effective boards will use methods like those discussed below in *Tactics: Strengthening experience and expertise*, to bring their roles into better balance with their non-executive colleagues.

We've noticed difficult dynamics emerging where boards are stuck in a particular long-term, out-of-kilter pattern. For instance, a founder who had moved into a non-executive chair position, at the insistence of shareholders, and who continued to exercise operational oversight. Relationship issues can also happen when boards suddenly shift towards a new balance of power. One member described being asked to step in as interim CEO on a board that he chaired, and once a replacement CEO was found, move back to his chair role. He told us how difficult and disorientating this was for everyone involved, and the conscious effort required to redraw and hold appropriate boundaries.

In such anxiety-inducing times, when board members' defences are raised, it's even more important to concentrate on relationships, although this may be the last thing you feel like doing. The chair of a government body shared some wise words *"If relationships are getting tense, you need to be spending more time together, not less. Which is so counter-intuitive ... It's uncomfortable, but it stops things bubbling up and surprising people."* She admitted that when she first became a chair, she thought it was just about chairing meetings. In reality, *"That's the tip of the iceberg. Underneath it's all about relationships and getting the most out of the team, rather than imagining you're chair, therefore you are better.*" Further, she counselled that if relations with some individuals are not 100%, then building relationships through others can help achieve the impact you seek. For example, working through board colleagues who have strong relationships with other members from whom you are more distant.

Crucial questions – Relating

- Where and how might you be misinterpreting each other (your behaviour and roles)?
- Where are the gaps in how you perceive your roles? How can you close these gaps?

We've just looked at ways to use clear role boundaries to find and maintain flexible alignment, and therefore trust between executive and non-executive board members. Another approach is to increase executive and non-executive experience to bolster confidence. This can reduce anxiety about the intentions and actions of others, and the defensive reactions it can cause.

Tactics: Strengthening experience and expertise

We've seen that holding power jointly requires mutual respect and understanding between executives and non-executives. One route to achieving this is appreciation of each other's experience and expertise. A common theme in our research was the importance of making sure you have a good balance of appropriate skills and knowledge around the table to achieve the goals of the board. One chair explains:

> *It means that when the board is discussing an issue, whether it's finance, marketing, communications or media, the rest of the board can see that a colleague is speaking from knowledge and experience. And can bring in "what ifs" and "for examples."*

This gives the board confidence that, during discussions, there's somebody who understands what they're talking about. Someone who can be supportive of the executive and be a critical friend. It creates a sense of security that enables more open and generative discussions. The conundrum is that having non-executives with deep knowledge of the organisation's industry can be a double-edged sword, leading to muscling in – as we outlined earlier. Our research surfaced two tactics for finding this delicate balance.

Learning from others

Encourage one-to-one discussions and relationships between executives and non-executives on areas of mutual expertise or experience. This helps both groups to deepen their understanding of each other's capacity to contribute. This is one element of building trust and in *Chapter 2: Negotiating the standoff*, we explore further advice on doing this. It's also valuable for executives to understand what it's like to be in a non-executive position. Our board veterans advocate practical steps to achieve this. One recommends that an aspiring CEO takes on a non-executive role first *"Because otherwise their only experience of a board is the one they're sitting on."* Whereas, if you're also a non-executive, *"You see it from their perspective rather than just from yours all the time."*

In psychological terms, this external experience can help CEOs stand in the shoes of their non-executive colleagues and think about things that might help and hinder them in the role. The shift in perspective can also prevent the misinterpretation of other people's actions. For example, one CEO felt disturbed by a non-executive colleague asking questions to which they already knew the answer. Was the non-executive trying to catch him out, or grandstanding? With no direct experience of a non-executive role in a regulated industry, the CEO did not recognise his colleague's well-meaning motivation to demonstrate compliance with a non-executive's fiduciary responsibility to probe and challenge. The non-executive simply wanted his question to be noted in the minutes as a tangible record of good governance – there was no ulterior motive to trip up the CEO. Experience on other boards could have made this CEO familiar, and more comfortable, with this common practice.

Moving within bounds

How can non-executives develop a better understanding of their executive colleagues' realities without undermining them? A senior non-executive director recommends allowing non-executives *"To move within the organisation and find out what they want – as long as they behave responsibly."* This means they can equip themselves to contribute without feeling excluded. Mutual agreement on clearly defined limits and ground rules is vital here for success. We explore this topic further in *Chapter 5: Descending the ivory tower*, where we describe the practical move of setting up a one-off, deep dive exercise. This investigation into a specific area, for a limited time, can be useful in situations where non-executives feel the anxiety, even unconsciously, of being shut out of a decision or area of enquiry.

In summary, building experience and expertise amongst executives and non-executives fosters mutual understanding. It enables board members to feel more equipped to raise and tackle difficult issues in constructive ways. Also, it can help to instil trust so they share power naturally and calmly, and feel able to surface and work through emotional tensions as they arise. As a board advisor with executive experience puts it, mutual understanding enables board members to deal with relationship issues that occur, rather than be caught up in the situation. *"You have to be the wise women or men. You have to be able to sit above that position, distance yourself and work with the anxiety and emotion."* That way, your board is less likely to be side-tracked by seesaw dynamics.

Crucial questions – Tactics

* How can you develop and use skills and knowledge to build trust and rebalance power?

A good way of attaining this position is to develop an environment where board members feel secure and free from defensive reactions – a psychologically safe boardroom.

Power tool: Psychological safety

Amy Edmondson of Harvard Business School made an accidental discovery while researching the impact of team work on medical error rates. She was initially surprised and disappointed to discover that more effective teams made more errors. Then she realised that the real difference was in the willingness of teams who worked effectively together to report errors. They were more likely to talk openly about errors and find new ways to catch and prevent them. She had stumbled across the impact of what Edgar Schein [11] identified as a climate of *psychological safety*. This enables people to focus on achieving shared goals, rather than protecting or defending themselves.

Edmondson defines psychological safety as "The belief that the work environment is safe for interpersonal risk taking. The concept refers to the experience of feeling able to speak up with relevant ideas, questions and concerns" [12]. She goes on to state that "psychological safety is present when colleagues trust and respect each other and feel able – even obligated – to be candid." In a board setting, the degree of psychological safety within the group is likely to affect the conscious and unconscious calculations made around the table. It will influence how secure members feel, how much they need to defend themselves. This in turn will impact what they feel they can and cannot say and do.

Improving psychological safety on a board can serve to lower these defences and improve relationships. How does a boardroom become more psychologically safe? Edmondson offers a simple, three-part toolkit. We outline it here and recommend Edmondson's book, *The Fearless Organisation* [12], together with the associated online resources such as Google's re:Work Guide to psychological safety [13].

Applying Edmondson's recommendations to board power sharing means:

- *Creating a learning environment*: setting the scene by framing board topics as learning problems, rather than execution problems, and emphasising why they matter. For example, instead of asking whether a pilot investment succeeded or failed, ask "What did we learn from that experiment?" and "How can we apply it to move faster on our sustainability goals?"
- *Inviting participation*: by creating time and space for board members to interact, in formal board meetings and other informal settings, and by asking genuine, curious and direct questions (with humility). This could mean using board time differently. For instance, limiting the number of agenda items to create time, and inviting full participation to explore an important dilemma for the organisation. We look further at inclusive decision-making in *Chapter 6: Harnessing diversity*.
- *Responding productively*: by listening carefully and showing appreciation of the contributions of others. In particular, by giving support and guidance to those who find the courage to say difficult things or bring bad news, and by clearly discouraging contributions which undermine trust and openness within the board.

These three principles play a vital role in creating the collaborative environment boards need to perform to their full potential. The chair has a significant role to play in building psychological safety within a board, but any member making a conscious choice to abide by these principles is also likely to evoke a change in the dynamic. The principles of psychological safety are a simple but tough discipline for individuals and boards, and can be a useful yardstick in board evaluation exercises. We investigate them in greater detail in the coming chapters.

Summary

Balancing power

Being on boards is psychologically challenging, because it's a high-stakes environment which requires a group to hold power together. Despite set roles and hierarchies, it may not be clear who is in charge. Power can shift, and this causes tensions. Boards with executives and non-executives must continually work to find and maintain a balance of power between themselves, over time.

Spotting the seesaw

It's a sign of seesaw dynamics when boundaries between roles are crossed without consent, and board members muscle into colleagues' territory. It's also a red flag when members pay lip service to collective responsibility within the boardroom, while undermining its authority and credibility elsewhere. Over time these seesaw dynamics may lead to board members questioning each other's competence and capability.

Psychological defences

The pressure of board work can trigger what psychodynamic psychologists call defence mechanisms. Psychological defences like *projection*, in which an individual ascribes their own difficult feelings to others, and *transference*, where someone transfers their feelings about a significant past figure onto another person in the present.

Psychological defences are unconscious, meaning board members are likely to be unaware that their behaviour is being influenced. People's defences trigger and interact with the defences of others, which can lead to difficult emotional dynamics.

The power-sharing structure, absence of role clarity and confusion about levels of work on boards, are also sources of psychological pressure and defensive responses.

Awareness: Explore your contribution

Use feedback and self-reflection to explore your own defensive reactions and the impact these might have on your colleagues and board dynamics.

Relating: Forge and maintain alignment

Develop and maintain clear, but flexible, mutual understanding about board roles and levels of work to generate alignment. Regular communication about these boundaries helps to balance power dynamics.

Tactics: Strengthen experience and expertise

Experience and expertise are sources of power. Actively encouraging learning from others about their roles, knowledge and skills is a good way to build mutual trust, confidence and respect between board members.

Power tool: Psychological safety

Creating a learning environment, inviting participation and supporting constructive contributions, improves levels of psychological safety in groups. It minimises psychological defences and in turn enables strong board performance.

Further reading

Why Do I Do That?: Psychological Defense Mechanisms and the Hidden Ways They Shape Our Lives by Joseph Burgo.

The Fearless Organization: Creating Psychological Safety in the Workplace for Learning, Innovation, and Growth by Amy Edmondson.

Coach and Couch: The Psychology of Making Better Leaders by Manfred Kets de Vries et al.

Chapter 2

Negotiating the standoff

I used to avoid conflict – I'd use collaborative skills, negotiation skills, building consensus skills, but I would avoid the conflict. I am getting to the point where now I'll let conflict happen and then bring out these well-established skills to manage it.

Charity chair and trustee, public sector body

Introduction

In the previous chapter we looked at the pressures arising from power sharing and managing boundaries between roles. Here we go further and consider a situation in which individuals or factions, with opposing views, are deadlocked in a standoff. Where common ground can't be found, and board members find themselves stuck in adversarial positions on a fundamental question. Whilst the problem on the table is usually an intellectual one, difficulties in tackling it commonly arise from uneasy relationships.

Differing views, forceful exchanges of opinion, even conflict, are naturally occurring features of groups of strong characters debating complex, potentially high-risk issues. In our experience, and for all the board members we interviewed, some friction is a desirable part of board dynamics. One charity trustee advised *"Don't be concerned by people taking stances. It's all part of the process and needs to happen to get to the right point."* Another director added that the board dynamic *"shouldn't be cosy at all – actually, it's good to have the grit in the oyster."* There needs to be a healthy tension *"otherwise you're just a group of yes men or women … You need somebody to present a very different opinion in order to sharpen your own thinking."*

But sometimes the conflict becomes too uncomfortable. Opposing forces become deadlocked over a significant issue, and it may feel impossible to find a way through the polarised debate. Over time, entrenched conflict like this can severely limit a board's ability to serve its purpose. As a veteran FTSE 100 board member spells out *"If there are bad dynamics and the board is fractious and seen*

DOI: 10.4324/9780429340239-4

as trouble, then the company can't do well. The candid but collegiate board is a must."

Another professional services board member graphically noted that it's usually the job of the chair to distinguish between *"lively debate, still all pointing in the right direction"* and *"actually we're not getting anywhere because people are just throwing rocks at each other."* Everyone on the board has a part to play in noticing and managing the conflict, as we'll see later.

What are the roots and nature of standoffs like this, and how can board members find a way forward? We examine the signals that relationship dynamics are coming to a standstill. We look inside a public sector boardroom, where dialogue was becoming impossible. Then we mine the work of psychoanalytic thought leaders Melanie Klein and Wilfred Bion, for insights into the psychological defence mechanisms at work, in individuals and groups, when people fall out. And we share techniques that board members, facilitators and coaches find effective to shift the group and unlock the organisation to move ahead.

What are you noticing? The board standoff

What are the warning signs that your board relationships maybe experiencing, or approaching, a standoff dynamic? Here are some common features identified by board members and their advisors.

No one is listening

The defining feature of standoffs experienced by our panel is that sides have been taken, and each side has lost the capacity to listen. This fundamental breach in communication is sure to stall progress. If no one is listening, it means no one is being heard and feelings of frustration and anger can simmer. In these situations, people on both sides focus their time and energy on reinforcing their own position and finding allies to stand alongside them. Around the boardroom table, at virtual or face-to-face meetings and in informal conversations, there is strong advocacy of firmly held views. What's missing is curiosity about other points of view, and a willingness to enquire into these, to really understand the perspective of others. We discuss how to cultivate these habits in the *Advice: Relating* section further down in this chapter.

Extreme views and feelings

In a disagreement, the act of taking sides can stir up further defensive feelings and impulses, as you experience threat and anticipate an attack. Let's assume that most people who reach board level are intelligent, well-intentioned and reasonable. So it's striking to hear board members describe those on the other side of their arguments as unreasonable, short-sighted or lacking intellect (and no doubt these colleagues might level the same insults at their accusers!).

It's as if board members, having taken sides, start to see their 'opposing' colleagues in a one-dimensional way. They are good or bad, a decision is right or wrong, an action will lead to success or failure. One board contemplating a venture into a new and highly regulated market found opinion swiftly splitting into for and against. Instead of tapping into sources of knowledge and expertise and weighing up their options, people seemed to have jumped to a firm yes or no response. Experience tells us that complex issues rarely have simple answers. The capacity to conjure with the nuanced grey, to find creative ways to resolve issues, is vital. But in standoff situations we take polarised, sometimes extreme, and often simplistic positions. And these are frequently accompanied by equally strong emotions, which don't always spring from the topic on the table.

Virtual back channels

These fierce emotions can be contagious and opposing sides sometimes establish informal channels that can amplify negative feelings. Traditionally, this was often done behind the scenes, one-to-one or in small group meetings. The rise of virtual and hybrid meetings means this behaviour can be accelerated by easy access to social messaging. One chair described the "*irritating and infectious*" habit of board members using private chat functions in virtual meetings. "*You see situations these days in meetings where people are emailing each other or texting each other – you get invited into it.*" This grows as members wind each other up and try to draw more people into their camp. In her view, these real-time back channels, running alongside formal meetings, are "*The worst form of private conversation you can possibly have in any meeting of people who are supposed to be governing the system.*"

They are also a sure sign of a deepening split into opposing groups – the basis of a standoff. Such private channels are often used to caricature and deride other positions and personalities. A public sector director described a troubled board on which people were becoming increasingly annoyed with each other. "*I think there are always some people who've got some personal foibles ... Whether that's saying something on a regular basis or how they shuffle their papers or the fact that they're always three minutes late.*" Colleagues can pick up these idiosyncrasies and ridicule them, establishing a culture of disrespect which can seep down through an organisation.

A siloed organisation

Standoffs cast a long shadow across an organisation because functions, teams and employees take their cues from the top. If the generals are drawing battle lines, the troops naturally fall in along them, and they may feel permitted, or even obliged, to engage in covert or overt sparring. This can be reflected lower down as silos, which operate totally independently or even vie against each other. In an outsourced services organisation, prolonged conflict at the top led to a situation where different parts of the firm stopped co-operating and began to compete, even pitching against each other in client tender processes. Clients, unsure whether the firm was poorly organised or enduring a political maelstrom, knew they were not looking at the competent, collaborative partner they were seeking. Boards which discuss the issue of silos, and how to improve collaboration amongst their staff, might do well to check in the mirror, because these situations can stem from a standoff dynamic within the board itself.

Finding it hard to break out

Finally, it's also clear how intractable these situations can feel from within. It's as if opposing sides are bound together, going round in exasperating circles or exerting effort in a tug of war. The experience of being in a deadlock seems to rob people of the ability to find creative ways to resolve it. Often it takes a board member, such as the chair, lead/senior independent director or a board advisor, to step outside the argument. To look at what's happening between people in the group and bring it calmly and repeatedly to the board's attention.

So far, we've explored several ways that you can notice a standoff. Table 2.1 is a summary of the common signs that indicate action is needed.

To examine stalemate situations and approaches to resolving them more deeply, let's look inside the boardroom of a public body. It was created to promote collaboration between disparate groups, but found itself struggling to find common ground.

Inside story: Uniting tribes

The chair of a government-commissioned independent body "*inherited a board of people who didn't want to be there.*" Most had been appointed because of their

Table 2.1 What are you noticing? The board standoff

Closed minds	People mostly communicate with those who agree with them and have stopped listening to others.
Factions	Individuals, pairs and splinter groups pursue their own agendas.
Extreme emotions	The emotional temperature seems fixed on boiling or freezing.
A stuck topic	Discussion goes round in increasingly acrimonious circles.
Polarised positions	Adamant thinking; the emergence of extreme solutions.
Lack of respect	Overt or convert personal attacks and caricaturing.
Back channels	Sub-groups develop secret informal communication channels.
Silos	Divisions at the top are replicated down through the organisation.

positions in public organisations and there was a statutory requirement to take part. Under duress, members assembled with the belief that "*Their job was to protect their patch. And so things became very difficult.*" On top of this, other members were there because their companies benefited from the contracts awarded by the body. As the chair recalled "*You can see a potential disaster in that.*"

He tried to begin a dialogue with this large and unwieldy board of 25 members, hampered by individuals often choosing to send deputies. It was a constantly changing cast of characters. The chair saw this as dangerous because they were not taking matters seriously. He also perceived them as "*determined to protect their own individual interests. Not thinking about the strategy*" for the board or the national objective they were trying to achieve. Those who did attend used absolutist language and made strident demands – insisting that their stakeholders must receive this or that. They also seemed to huddle in groups, in echo chambers reinforcing their own positions and deriding those of their "*opponents.*" Different factions responded to each other's requests and observations with scorn and ridicule.

The chair deduced it was crucial to agree a strategy "*However thorny the road to getting there.*" He'd experienced a lack of clear direction on previous boards and determined to use the device of a unifying strategy here. He confided that this was "*A way of overcoming what I thought was the most dreadful board dynamics.*"

> *Of course having a strategy anyway is important in its own right. But I did use it as a way of getting people to focus on why we were all there together. And as a way of ensuring that resources could be directed towards those in greatest need.*

The path proved particularly thorny. Members were second-guessing the impact of strategic agreements on their own patch and positioning themselves accordingly. Factions formed amongst members with similar interests, as people sought strength in numbers to protect themselves, and these groups went into battle against each other. The strategy process became increasingly acrimonious, with members questioning each other's integrity. Decisions could not be made, and two particularly forthright members ganged up against the chair. He began to receive formal complaints from the two (who aligned their agendas), alleging that conflicts of interest had been improperly handled. Also, he became aware that information from board meetings was leaking into the press – to the consternation of the government department which had appointed him. The last straw was an article in a trade publication accusing the chair of bias in his role, which could only have come from within the board.

Before we recount what happened next, let's look at what might cause a group assembled to work on a shared task to undermine their own efforts so spectacularly. We turn first to the psychoanalyst Melanie Klein, who built on the Freuds' work on defence mechanisms (discussed in Chapter 1). Her ideas shed light on reasons why board members, under pressure, might defend themselves from uncomfortable feelings in ways which lead to relationship rifts. Then we explore the ideas of Wilfred Bion, who investigated the difficulties humans experience when put into group situations.

Psychological roots: From fighting each other to teaming up to succeed

Splitting into right and wrong

Klein used close observation of young children at play to devise theories that illuminate why we might become so single-minded in standoff situations, and so wedded to a point of view, course of action, person or place in an organisation. Her theories are wide ranging and rich, but here we cherry pick one that was core to her view of the human psyche – *splitting*. From her research, Klein deduced that as an infant, our earliest relationships involve intense feelings, both pleasurable and painful. To cope, we split our very early experiences into good and bad, which we handle in different ways to protect our developing sense of self from threatening feelings of anxiety.

According to Klein, as a young child we then project these good and bad feelings onto things or people around us. Remember how we described the defence mechanism of projection in Chapter 1? This type of projection involves distancing ourselves from split feelings by attributing them to other people or objects, dividing the world around us into good and bad. This is an important step in learning to interact with the world around us, and developing an understanding of our place in relation to it [14]. She noticed that older children who are telling stories or playing imaginative games tend to create heroes and villains. Characters to hate and fear, and ones to love and idolise. Given the success of the Marvel, DC and Star Wars franchises, for example, it seems that splitting the world in this way is appealing to adults too!

Crucially for leaders, Klein believed that at times of great "*persecutory anxiety*," adults regress to early methods like splitting. To protect ourselves from distressing and ambiguous feelings, we split things, people and decisions into right and wrong. Klein's work then suggests that internal conflicts can be relieved by taking a part of our split off feelings and ascribing them to people or objects around us. This is usually the part we perceive as bad, such as an urge to destroy a person standing in our way. We strongly identify with one side of an argument and ascribe the other extreme to our adversaries, whom we see as wrong.

When a board is divided in a standoff, individual members may be using the defence of splitting to deal with the extreme discomfort of being unsure what to do for the best. This can involve over-simplification of a multi-faceted strategic question into a binary right and wrong answer. You might think of it as black and white thinking, where the only options an individual seems capable of entertaining are two polarised extremes. For example, should you focus on global reach or local touch? Should you lead on quality or price? Do you need to make investments or cuts? This either/or mindset enables the individual to take a strong position on what they see as the right side. Then they locate their board colleagues on the other side of the argument, and characterise their position as extreme and fundamentally wrong.

Creating an enemy

A classic example of this, from our private equity interviews, is a founder who has accepted funds from an investor and, as part of the deal, agrees to some level of control by them. After a honeymoon period, this control starts to chafe, and eventually feels completely unacceptable to the founder. At a rational level, the founder knows it's all in the contract, but they fervently wish to get out from under it. So they split off this uncomfortable feeling of not wanting to keep their side of the deal, and locate the feeling in the investor firm. They develop a sense that the investor is untrustworthy and doesn't want to keep their side of the deal. Or in the words of one interviewee "*Private equity always wants to screw founders.*"

Our inside story public sector body board also looks like the perfect environment to trigger its members' unconscious defences against the threat of personally painful experiences. Members who are representatives of other public bodies are likely to feel a strong allegiance to their own organisation, which trumps their loyalty to the government-commissioned body and its board. So each member is there to make decisions in the best interests of the public, but is also strongly motivated to protect the interests of their own tribe. This conflict of interests generates a painful moral dilemma that is not easily resolved, and leads individuals to view others as enemies.

In *Why Do I Do That?* [10], Joseph Burgo's useful book about defence strategies, he pinpoints the problem with seeing other people as simply wrong. It comes at a great cost in terms of our ability to explore or be curious about the position of colleagues on the other side of the argument. We are unaware that the enemy is within, and our unconscious determination to defend our own 'right' side stops us from listening and seeking to understand. We prevent ourselves from being open to finding creative ways to resolve the impasse. It's a powerful bind.

Being hijacked by unconscious assumptions

The psychoanalyst Wilfred Bion trained with Klein and brought a radical new angle to the analysis of defence mechanisms in groups of people. From observing groups of convalescing soldiers in hospital during the Second World War, he saw psychological defence mechanisms operating, not just within and between people, but as emergent properties of the groupings themselves. He was particularly interested in the struggles that result from these group defences. Bion noted

> It is clear that when a group forms, the individuals forming it hope to achieve some satisfaction from it. It is also clear that the first thing they are aware of is a sense of frustration produced by the presence of the group of which they are members.

> [15]

According to Bion, in every group there are often two groups present, psychologically speaking. The *work group* at the conscious, logical level and the *basic assumption group* at the unconscious, emotional level. The work group is focused on the task the group has formed to perform – he called this the *primary task*. For a board, this is likely to be directing the organisation whilst protecting shareholder or stakeholder interests. The American psychotherapist Margaret Rioch points out that attention to this task can keep a board grounded and allow them to operate in sophisticated, rational ways, despite the unconscious forces of the basic assumption group [16].

Bion's theories suggest that when the board is under pressure, directors may become unwittingly obsessed by their emotional needs, at the expense of the business in hand. They are driven by their unconscious basic assumptions. We might think of a basic assumption as an instinct, which shows up as a shared emotional state when a group perceives a threat. Whilst we are not consciously aware of these motivating basic assumptions, we nonetheless act, individually and collectively, as if they are vital to our safety and survival. Like culture in an organisation, they define correct behaviour, organise status and shape interactions. Unfortunately, they also draw attention, energy and focus away from the group's core work purpose, undermining the job of the board.

One director described how, in practice, we can entertain high levels of friction and discord in a board, and it can remain very functional – as long as all members are aiming at the same high-level objectives. It's tricky when "*The psychologies and the politics have a life of their own, which has nothing to do with the objectives of the organisation. That's when they become completely dysfunctional.*" This is when, in Bion's terms, board group behaviour is driven by its unconscious basic assumptions. Bion's great insight is to notice that people in groups have an attraction, or in his words *valency*, towards one of three types of fundamental emotional basic assumptions: *fight-flight*, *pairing* and *dependency*. We'll look at the first two of these here, and you can read about the third in *Chapter 3: Banishing bullying*.

Fight or flight

The first basic assumption is that the group must be preserved, and Bion observes that this instinct can send groups into fight or flight mode [15]. The board, as a group in this mindset, needs an enemy, which can be found outside or inside the boardroom. In a psychological manoeuvre, which echoes Klein's concept of splitting, the group identifies a foe and then focuses its attention on attacking or defending against its perceived aggressor. In this state, a sense of threat or peril has triggered an unconscious feeling in the group that it must fight the predator or flee from the danger it represents.

A board which has splintered into warring factions might be influenced by the instinct to fight to protect the group and locate the enemy inside the board. Here the culture of the board is likely to be belligerent (witness the factional disputes in our independent body inside story). In this mode, board members' thoughts tend towards attack and defence, as the sympathetic nervous system continually prepares their bodies for action. We look at the neuroscience of this in Part Three. In this state, it's difficult for people to engage rationally, creatively and openly with the real tasks in front of them. The stage is set for aggressive behaviour, short-term thinking and rash decisions.

In contrast, groups in flight mode find less aggressive ways to divert themselves from the work in hand. From inconsequential chit-chat to preoccupation with minor issues or irrelevant initiatives, the flight group contrives to avoid the real work of the board. Individuals and the group firmly resist attempts to refocus on any activity which serves the explicit purpose of the board. Perhaps in our inside story, members sending stand-ins to the board, and those seeking to subvert the decision-making process, were in flight mode. Both tactics neatly prevented the board from addressing the central task it needed to accomplish.

Pairing

The second unconscious basic assumption experienced by a group is perhaps the most obvious, but it's rarely acknowledged in the world of work. This is the preoccupation with a pair of people in a group's midst. From our first days at school, when we looked hopefully for someone who might be a best friend, to later quests for life partners or collaborators on important endeavours, the urge to bond in pairs lies deep within us. We associate pairs with generating new life and creating opportunities. When couples form on boards, they are closely observed and commented upon. Joshua Wolf Shenk investigates this phenomenon in *Powers of Two* [17], in which he observes the innovative nature of creative pairs. It's a fascinating delve into the chemistry at the heart of long-term partnerships – John Lennon and Paul McCartney, Marie and Pierre Curie, Steve Jobs and Steve Wozniak.

According to Bion, when groups are under pressure, they look unconsciously to a pair's creativity to save the group from their problems and generate answers. In our research, we've seen boardroom pairs who seem so close that they are almost joined at the hip. Close, productive partnerships meld and gel, sometimes travelling within or to other organisations together (one might move to a new role and be swiftly followed by the other). We've also noticed the 'work spouse' phenomenon. A mutually supportive and often affectionate relationship between a pair of colleagues, which over time comes to mirror a marriage. One founder openly refers to his CEO as his work-wife and notes that they spend more time together than with either actual spouse. Our research does not record the reactions of their actual life-partners!

Opposites can also attract. We have worked with several long-standing CEO and CFO pairs with diametrically opposed personality types and operating styles, but a willingness and ability to appreciate the value of each other's approach. Whatever the set-up, the 'pairs' basic assumption in boards can also be divisive, as the rest of the group waits for the CEO and chair, or specific pairs of directors or trustees, to show the way forward. The group may become passive or complacent, like the boards in Part Two of this book, as they cede power to a dynamic duo. In our inside story, the paired board members are secretly briefing the press and making complaints to bring things to a head. In this situation, perhaps the pair aim to appoint a new CEO or chair to create new leadership and direction. Others may condone or actively support their efforts, as a solution to the anxious and stressful position they find themselves in – rather than take steps to enable the board to do its work and focus on its primary task.

The unconscious ebb and flow

Groups, including boards, are likely to move between focusing on their work, and finding their efforts and attention hijacked by the basic assumptions of flight or flight, pairing or dependency. (We'll return to dependency, which involves searching for a protector, in the next chapter.) The basic assumptions ebb and flow, dominating at different times within a group. Everyone in the group is unwittingly complicit in the prevailing basic assumption. Should individuals challenge this, what Bion calls the *group mentality* is brought to bear on them in uncomfortable ways. People in the group feel pressure to conform to the prevailing assumption, although none of the group members are aware of applying this pressure.

This leads us to consider what can be done when a split board is in fight mode, fleeing from its problems, or stuck waiting for a pair to produce a solution. How can the group manage its emotional anxiety and defensive responses, so they return to their work task? Let's re-join our government body inside story to discover how they made progress.

Inside story: What happened next?

The independent body chair, who had been driven to distraction by the factions in his membership, decided to do three things. First, he offered his resignation to the board because they had genuinely lost confidence in him. In an honest and uncomfortable speech to the group, he described the dynamic as he saw it. He pointed out the impossibility of getting anything done and reaffirmed his commitment to the overarching goal the body had been set up to achieve. His offer was declined by the board. Next, he faced up to the rumbling grievances by saying "*If you think someone is corrupt, then lodge an official complaint.*" He was pretty sure that there was no real case, but he wanted to take this group, which was in the grip of a fight basic assumption, to the brink of all out warfare. No official complaint was forthcoming.

Finally, he worked with his board colleagues to establish a set of cross-factional, issue-based working groups. These were tasked with exploring a particular issue together, rather than coming up with concrete conclusions. Working in smaller groups enabled less adversarial, more attuned interactions. Pursuit of understanding, rather than answers, lowered the stakes between members sufficiently, so they were able to start listening to each other. Inviting people to focus on the primary task or work objectives at hand served to defuse tensions. This chair's thoughtful words for boards in conflict are "*Try and find a way of introducing something into the boardroom which helps people to understand the context within which the rows are taking place*" because this can "*engender mutual understanding of paths towards shared goals.*"

It wasn't a miracle cure, but the board did reach a point where they could agree a strategy for achieving the objectives for which they were responsible.

So how can you bring your board back together in standoff situations?

Advice on negotiating a standoff

Awareness: Managing yourself

In Chapter 1 we covered advice on exploring your impact, and this holds good for standoff situations too. It's a useful first step to ask yourself how your choices, interactions and responses might be reinforcing the dynamic. Where there's conflict, one chair advises you to be aware of your personality, and how you approach things. Do you tend to avoid confrontation and keep tensions under wraps? Or are you someone who likes to get issues out and thrash them through to move on? We've talked above about the psychology of ways that individuals respond to disagreements and tensions, as well as the dynamics that can arise at group level. You can use both levels of awareness in the moment, to check how you are contributing to the dynamic and find a different perspective on the situation. This opens up options for a change of tack from your usual default approach, to shift a stuck dynamic. Here we look at the next step. How you can use this kind of awareness to manage yourself and consciously alter your impact – for example, to break a deadlock.

Beginning at group level, it's interesting, as a CEO, chair or board member, to step back, particularly in emotionally tense situations, and see whether you can spot any of Bion's basic assumptions at work. You might catch a glimpse of a group urge to fight, take flight from the task in hand or position a pair as the answer to your problems. If your board is currently in the grip of one of these basic assumptions, what is that like for you, and what is the effect on your board and its work? It's intriguing to observe what happens if you point out to your board colleagues the basic assumption that you have spotted operating in the boardroom.

Turning to self-awareness, a director in a local authority described acting on useful advice from a board colleague early in her career. This colleague observed that, in difficult situations, the director tended to be, not defensive exactly, but "*to push back a bit.*" She was inclined to take sides in an argument quickly and firmly, splitting her board colleagues into allies and adversaries. He reminded her that's fine, but there are times where a "*bit of a pause*" would be helpful to consider the points of view of others. She now bears this in mind in work interactions, including with boards and executive leadership groups. Making changes like this may well need practice. Another director admits the need to prompt himself to avoid being too opinionated and to seek the views of others.

> *I've made big mistakes when I thought I knew, and I was so certain I just bulldozed my way through. A more senior colleague said once that he'd never been to a committee that hadn't improved the outcome, and I have to remind myself of that.*

This helps him to keep an open mind.

To break a standoff dynamic, at least one side is going to have to move. They don't necessarily have to give in, but rather to change their position sufficiently to elicit a different response from the opposing side. As we discussed in the introduction, if you want a situation to change, this usually means choosing to do something differently yourself, as you're in control of your own actions (not those of others). Altering your perspective on your own and others' points of view can be your starting point for resolving a standoff. In their excellent book *Simple Habits for Complex Times* [18], Jennifer Garvey Berger and colleagues recommend a powerful habit which can be very useful when you find yourself in stuck arguments. She advocates asking "How might I be wrong?" It's an invitation to manage your human desire to be right, by considering what you might be missing. Might the enemy be within you, as we discussed earlier? What haven't you really understood yet, and crucially how might the same situation look from other perspectives? Here's how our board members and their advisors enquire into other perspectives to resolve standoffs.

Crucial questions – Awareness

- How might I be wrong?
- What might I be missing?

Relating: Seeking first to understand

The following wise words are one of Stephen Covey's habits from *The Seven Habits of Highly Effective People*, his classic leadership book. He points out that "Most people do not listen with the intent to understand; they listen with the intent to reply" [19]. Covey notes the human tendency to assume that the person you disagree with hasn't understood you and to rush in to correct them, rather than wondering if there is something you haven't understood yourself. He counsels "If you wish to be understood, you first need to understand." If you don't seek to understand, one veteran chair warns about "*communicating out of fear.*" You can become anxious and manage this by putting up barriers and resorting to the type of split thinking and feeling we discussed earlier. This chair has seen colleagues taking the attitude towards others of "*I don't want to hear what they've got to say, so best just don't ask them.*" Seeking first to understand is a great antidote to this. In our interviewees' experience it has several elements.

Stopping and making space

To really understand, an experienced chair observes that "*You've got to give people the time of day*" and be comfortable that they are "*allowed to disagree with you.*" The sage advice is to simply stop and listen. This means having respect for others and their positions and assuming they come with genuine intentions. Another expert chair of trustees observes that colleagues

> *May have differences in personalities. They may have some conflicts, but by and large they're trying to do the right thing. So, you do well to listen to others who have a different perspective to yours to hear what their story is.*

He reminds us that there's genuine truth to the phrase "*You have two ears and one mouth and you should use them in that ratio.*" Just listen to others for a while, without being defensive. "*Don't just do something, stand there.*"

Being curious

Curiosity and an open mind are also important elements of seeking to understand. They help you find out where others are coming from, and why they hold the views that they do. A director who noticed that skills from her previous career were useful on boards, says that as a probation officer "*I would want to find out as much about the person I'm working with as possible.*" What else about their life is really important? "*Without knowing those things, how can I possibly help to enable them to make the changes they need to make.*" This director applied the same rules to working alongside board colleagues. "*I suppose that nosiness, that curiosity, has served me very well.*" She also observed that good boards "*don't need to score points*" but are intrigued by each other's views. It's good to pursue your curiosity about another position in a debate, until you can articulate it convincingly to someone else. We give an example of how this can work in the *Advice: Tactics* section further down in this chapter.

Having empathy

Once you've endeavoured to understand your board colleagues' perspectives, you can go one step further and feel empathy about other things that might be going on in their lives. Take the example of the board member who feels tired and unprepared for meetings, and automatically takes an inflexible stance to conserve energy. This means they don't have to think things through or risk being shown up. We explore further the nature and impact of this automatic thinking in Part Two and Part Three. The CEO of an international charity urges that every colleague is human, and you need to "*walk in other people's shoes. When people are being a bit grumpy, they probably haven't read the board papers and they don't know what to say when somebody asks them for their opinion.*" They might have woken at five in the morning, after a broken night's sleep with a new baby. It's important to be conscious of this, and be aware that another time it could be you in this type of situation. Since we largely don't know what's going on behind the scenes for other people, and how this might be affecting them, it's best to express understanding. This improves relationships and begins to build trust.

Crucial questions – Relating

- How can I be curious to really understand?
- What is it like to be my colleague?

Building trust up front

Virtually everyone we interviewed stressed the critical importance of trust within a board, to enable healthy conflict, minimise standoffs and ward off the basic assumptions of fight and flight and pairing. A director of a FTSE 100 company explains "*Boards don't work well if the board members think that their job is to turn up for meetings, to fulfil the terms of reference of the board or that board committee. And then go home and think nothing about it until the next board committee meeting.*"

That sort of transactional, task-focused environment, where relationships aren't nurtured, can potentially stoke the standoff fire. *"You've got to have this broader view"* of your board colleagues to truly comprehend and be able to work with the dynamics of the group.

A number of interviewees advocated investing in group activities like away-days, dinners, board evaluations and brain-storming sessions to strengthen group trust. Ideally face-to-face, but if that's not possible you can go a surprisingly long way virtually. This allows time to share personal stories and histories which, as we saw in the previous section, are so important. Particularly when new board members join, insight into each other's personality preferences, likes and dislikes, interests and passions help a board develop trust. This can reduce the chance of splits and help to heal rifts that are beginning to open up. But what if you're already past the point where there is an appetite for mutual understanding or trust-building? How can you take steps to bring the sides of a split board back together? As we saw in our inside story, a key approach is looking for areas where everyone agrees.

Tactics: Finding common ground

Finding a common purpose

Bion's experiments with therapeutic communities made him certain of one thing: a group needs a common purpose to ground it and avoid unconscious subversion of its efforts. This is the primary task we mentioned earlier. In Bion's field work, the hospital community needed to acknowledge and understand their mental illness and turn their attention to improving their psychological states. For a board, the situation might be about achieving a particular goal or creating something, or defeating a common enemy like a competitor or global problem. A private sector senior independent director explains *"Most people can align themselves around a common external objective that is the one unifying thing. There's an existential threat in all businesses, all of the time, which does tend to focus the mind."*

What does this look like in practice? This director describes responding to internal disputes between colleagues by reflecting on their situation like this: *"I hear what you're saying, but let's turn our focus externally rather than internally, because internally you will always find a way to disagree."* It's about finding a cause around which board members can coalesce, such as keeping customers or stakeholders happy. *"So, if you can try and unite people around something then you're halfway there ... building from a point of view of consensus rather than conflict."* This might be about pulling together to address a shared problem or teaming up to take advantage of an opportunity.

Another chair of an academic body uses a similar tactic to break down ingrained conflict between different parts of the institution. They found that academics on the board often had their first allegiance to the department that enabled their discipline to flourish. This led to a board level standoff between departments seeking to protect their own interests. "*The trick is to get them to realise that by being loyal to the university you are loyal to your discipline and your students. Encourage loyalty to something bigger than yourself.*" When this happens the discussion can move from what or who is right or wrong, to "*What's best right now for the whole organisation?*" The need for common purpose and shared goals explains the fundamental importance of vision and strategy to boards. Beyond agreeing how best to generate value, they play an important psychological role in uniting the board and giving them a common touchstone. Although this is not without potential pitfalls, it's a beacon to follow, particularly in times of extreme emotional pressure.

Crucial questions – Tactics

- What is our primary task as a board and how can we make progress on it?

Preparing the ground

Many commented that preparing the ground first, so that board members are alive to potential issues, is an important skill in resolving a standoff. The process is likely to be a series of one-to-one, sub-group and whole-group discussions. Investment of time before and between these meetings is crucial for managing constructive conflict. One chair explains that when the board was negotiating vexed issues "*I always made a point of ringing each member up before a board meeting and saying: 'You've seen the agenda, anything particularly worrying you, anything you want to raise?'*" He could then anticipate the views of a group beforehand and prepare his tactics for dealing with them.

He goes on to advise that, in times of change and conflict, it's best to "*Be very careful about collegiate relationships – stress them even more. Prepare people more ahead of time for changes in direction or proposals you want to take ... don't surprise them out of the blue.*" This sort of preparation minimises the likelihood of the board getting triggered into an unconscious emotional basic assumption at the expense of the work in hand. A serial chair described narrowing complex problems down into simple, important components, then working out which people are involved or need to move, and helping them reach agreement by asking "*We're here, we want to get there, how do we do that?*" This chair wasn't interested in scoring points or winning arguments. They kept their focus on finding a way to "*move on to the next step.*"

Naming the dynamic

When it feels hard to move to the next step, an executive in a global technology company advocates raising the problem – of being stuck in a standoff – for discussion. "*Don't try to solve it, just work with your observations.*" By this she means that going in with a judgement on the problem, or a solution to fix the situation, is unlikely to be productive. Instead, observe the situation carefully, and reflect what you are noticing back into the group. For example, in a group that had reached an impasse on a difficult question, she drew attention to this in a calm and measured way, without pointing the finger of blame at anyone. She simply said

> *I notice that when we speak about this topic people become quite watchful of each other. And that I don't say what I think, because I know it might set off another round of the argument we had last time, which I found very uncomfortable. Nonetheless, I do want to talk about it.*

She asked if the group wanted to have the discussion, and what might enable a constructive exchange of opinions. She had discovered that naming the dynamic in a tense situation is often a surprisingly good way of defusing it and opening up the possibility of finding common ground.

Engaging external support

Boards frequently draw on external consultants, facilitators or coaches to shape and facilitate the process of breaking an impasse. A chair describes a useful technique he learnt from a board evaluation and development specialist. Although the chair had felt it was normally his role to make interjections and observations during meetings, in the midst of entrenched positions his "*head was unfortunately probably 80% consumed by the topic itself.*" The specialist facilitator was able to be more detached, and when observing a board meeting, stopped the discussion and shared that she noticed two groups of directors start "*to build their castles of opinions.*" Positions were polarised and they were just reinforcing the point of view which they had already shared 15 minutes earlier. The facilitator helped them notice this and suggested how to snap out of it in a smart way. She proposed that "*people, instead of explaining their opinion, could say what they heard from the other side*" and this "*completely changed the dynamic.*" In meetings since, members have been more likely to notice when this is happening, and now have a simple, shared technique which they can use to break a deadlock.

External support can bring a fresh pair of eyes and a genuinely objective perspective, as well as practical tools and techniques to shift behaviours. Some advisors have specific processes or sets of principles which they use in standoff or conflict situations. Below we look at a particularly useful framework for managing conflict within a board.

Power tool: Orchestrating the conflict

This framework for managing conflict comes from a highly rated book on adaptive leadership called *Leadership on the Line: Staying Alive Through the Dangers of Leading*, by Ronald Heifetz and Marty Linsky [20]. It's a useful group intervention, particularly for a chair, senior or lead director or external facilitator. The authors, one formerly a clinical psychiatrist and the other with a background in law and politics, believe that "to lead is to live dangerously" [20]. They point out that whenever you tackle a tough issue there will be conflict, and it's the role of leaders to reduce the destructive potential. In our experience, this applies equally to board members. The authors' advice for doing this is four-fold.

Create a holding environment

A holding environment is like a container that is strong enough to hold the emotions that emerge when a group has an important conversation about something that really matters. For board groups, this discussion could be about the fight or flight or pairing basic assumptions, or fiercely held extreme positions. The container is a safe time and place for tackling tough, divisive questions, in ways in which everyone can actively participate. It should enhance the board's feelings of psychological safety, which we discussed in Chapter 1.

Reflecting actively and practically on what might create feelings of safety for a particular board, and the people it comprises, is important in setting up a supportive holding environment. Perhaps the venue makes a difference, or the way an agenda is shaped and a topic framed within it. Maybe the chair needs to give specific permissions or undertakings. Or model a certain kind of mindset or behaviour that encourages others to follow suit. For example, they may need to demonstrate a genuine commitment to ensuring everyone is heard.

Control the temperature

Next be aware of how you can dial up the emotional heat with provocation and challenge. This can enable the group to surface issues and feel the weight of responsibility. Sense when you might lower it by using tactics like breaking problems down, seizing simple wins and sharing green shoots of success. Or by using humour and appealing to shared values and purpose. Key to doing this is being aware and in control of your own emotional temperature, and carefully monitoring that of the board. The aim is to keep the temperature high enough to galvanise the team, but not so hot as to cause a meltdown.

The chair in our inside story was doing this. He turned up the temperature by offering his resignation and kept it at a rolling boil by inviting people with complaints to lodge them publicly. His working groups brought the stakes and the temperature back down. They served to dissect the problems, and set the conditions for mutual exploration and understanding of the underlying issues within a broad context.

Pace the work

Let issues develop, ideas percolate and understanding build. Some issues will need to come to the board many times, in different guises, before you find a sustainable response that everyone can get behind. During this process, individuals and the group need to be prepared to improvise, adapt and overcome.

Many of our interviewees talked about the time and patience it takes to move a tricky board situation forward, including carefully choreographed calls and conversations paced with sensitivity and determination. Trying to push in a straight line to resolve a multi-faceted issue is likely to be less effective than maintaining steady momentum. This can be generated by giving people time to make sense of the situation, come around to different viewpoints, and enable a sustainable way forward to emerge.

Show them the future

Keep referring back to the board's common purpose, just as Bion and our board tacticians advise. Use the vision and strategy, and concrete manifestations of these, to describe the 'dream.' Keep talking about the future as you hope to see it – the thing worth fighting for. Publicly welcome early signs of progress, to encourage the board to keep moving in a shared direction.

Summary

Standoffs arise from defensive instincts

Boards experiencing a standoff find themselves locked in adversarial positions on a fundamental question. This can happen due to unconscious psychological defences evoked by conflict. In stalemate situations, members have stopped listening to each other and may have taken up extreme positions to which they are emotionally attached. Factions have formed and these divisions may be reflected down through the organisation. It feels like an impasse – neither side wants to budge.

Relocating the enemy

Splitting is a concept from psychodynamic psychology. It describes a powerful unconscious mechanism, used by individuals when they feel under attack, to protect their sense of identity by dividing experiences into good and bad. We sometimes create a safe distance from bad feelings by locating them in others, setting up emotionally charged standoff dynamics. There's a further uncomfortable truth: the very membership of a group causes frustrations in people, borne of their collective fears and anxieties. This can trigger unconscious, defensive cultures, beliefs and patterns of behaviour on boards, such as pairing and fight and flight behaviours.

Awareness: Manage yourself

Face up to your own defensive role in a standoff dynamic and take responsibility for finding a way to resolve the group conflict. This takes resolve, patience, creativity and the capacity to lean into uncomfortable situations and question how you might be mistaken or missing something. Most of all, it takes courage.

Relating: Seek first to understand

Listen to others with care. Making time for people and genuinely seeking to understand them has the potential to transform a standoff dynamic. It's important to really tap into your empathy for others and their point of view, with deep curiosity.

Tactics: Search for common ground

People need common ground to resolve splits and fights, so it's vital to find this. Ideally a board builds trust early. If it's lacking, spend time together finding the uniting purpose for a shared way ahead.

Power tool: Orchestrating the conflict

Conflict needs to be skilfully facilitated to harness its creative potential with the minimum of collateral damage. Orchestrate the conflict by creating a supportive environment for debating views, gauging when to hold back or challenge, and giving board members time to process ideas. It's important to keep refocusing on your common purpose and shared future. Anyone on a board can find themselves with a role to play in managing conflict to resolve a standoff. It requires tolerance and tenacity to put your head above the parapet for the good of the organisation.

Further reading

Simple Habits for Complex Times: Powerful Practices for Leaders by Jennifer Garvey Berger and Keith Johnston.
Experience in Groups by Wilfred Bion.
Dynamics at Boardroom Level: A Tavistock Primer for Leaders, Coaches and Consultants by Leslie Brissett, Mannie Sher and Tazi Lorraine Smith.
Leadership on the Line: Staying Alive Through the Dangers of Leading by Ronald Heifetz and Marty Linsky.

Chapter 3

Banishing bullying

You want some forceful people on a board. And life being what it is those force-ful people often get into the most authoritative positions on the board where it's easier for them to bully.

CEO, digital mental health business

Introduction

Whether you think of it as coercive, dominant behaviour or downright bullying, the misuse of a position of power – to undermine or control others – is as old as the hills. Whatever term we use, there is no doubt that board members sometimes experience their colleagues as bullies, and this casts a long shadow. Feeling bullied can be painful and damaging for individuals, relationships, and the ability of the board to perform. An unchecked bully at the helm also sets an unethical tone within an organisation, sending strong signals about what is permissible within its culture. With the price of bullying so high, why does the dynamic persist?

The history of public, private and third sector organisations is peppered with coercive characters. Figures like Robert Maxwell, the publisher and CEO of the Mirror Newspaper Group in the UK, and Macmillan Publishers in the USA, who was renowned for his domineering tactics during the 1980s and 1990s. A charis-matic, ruthless and imposing individual, he had a reputation for sacking editors on the spot, by his own admission *"like a thunderclap"* [21]. Such was his everyday power over people that one of our interviewees remembers watching board mem-bers stand up to attention as Maxwell entered the room.

There are excellent explorations into the psyches of domineering leaders, and what causes them to behave this way. However, there is less investigation into how boardroom bullies get away with their evidently unacceptable behaviour. On his death in disputed circumstances in 1991, Maxwell left £400 million in debts. To shore up his businesses, he had misappropriated money from the news-paper group's pension fund and deprived 33,000 people of their pensions [22]. According to subsequent government investigations, many of his fellow directors

DOI: 10.4324/9780429340239-5

and professional advisers had simply failed to spot his unethical practices, or were slow to take action to curb them [23]. So why do board members in situations like this fail to challenge bullies in their midst?

In this chapter we examine why colleagues are often reluctant to act. We explore some more psychodynamic theories that help explain the reasons for this bystanding behaviour, and ways to overcome it. Our interviewees provide advice on managing overbearing board members. Ways to banish the behaviour rather than the person – if that's feasible – and what can be done if it's not.

Let's look first at how bullying might come about, and the roles of key players in this dynamic.

Noticing bullying

What is bullying? Extreme coercive behaviour is clearly bullying, but in other cases it's a grey area which has a subjective element. One person's impassioned discussion can be another person's overbearing aggression. One pragmatic definition of bullying, which concentrates on its impact, is provided by Acas, the UK Advisory, Conciliation and Arbitration Service. It describes workplace bullying as "unwanted behaviour from a person or group that is either offensive, intimidating, malicious or insulting, or an abuse or misuse of power that undermines, humiliates, or causes physical or emotional harm to someone." We think this is a useful definition for boards, as it focuses on evaluating the impact of the behaviour on the individual, which is the best gauge. Acas points out that it can be "a regular pattern of behaviour or a one-off incident." It can happen face-to-face, on social media, in emails or calls, and may not always be obvious or noticed by others [24].

We look in turn at the roles of the boardroom bully, their victims and the bystanders who witness this dynamic playing out.

Our interviewees reported seeing a spectrum of behaviour that they classified as bullying, summarised in Table 3.1. The most overt bullies were described as a *"toxic radio-active force"* and *"incredibly disruptive."* Macho terms were often

Table 3.1 Hallmarks of bullying behaviour

Overbearing arrogance.
Aggression.
Emotional outbursts.
Playing manipulative games.
Closing others down.
Public belittling.
Private undermining.

used to convey their attitudes: "*ruling the roost*," "*Rottweiler-like*" or "*bully boy*," although not all bullies described were male. Others detailed bullying that was less obvious, but nonetheless damaging in its impact.

There are some features of bullying, which you might see happening blatantly, or in more subtle ways. Overbearing arrogance is a common theme in our research, often anchored seemingly in the bully's sense of intellectual superiority, or other forms of inflated self-belief. One established director saw it as power going to their colleague's head. Such colleagues were described as pontificating, dominating discussion and treating colleagues in dismissive and condescending ways. Tactics included continually accusing other board members of not being commercial enough, or being overly sensitive in their responses.

Open aggression – erupting in angry outbursts – was another theme. There were boards where a member routinely shouted at others, swore and used language some found inappropriate. Colleagues, most frequently a chair or CEO, could be openly hostile "*Having a go at someone who can't fight back, using the power of the role.*" Fellow directors were told by one non-executive director "*If you were in my business, I would fire you.*" This non-executive asked questions in "*an unpleasant way, using offensive language. They indicated that they mistrusted the executives, that the executives didn't know what they were doing.*"

There were also examples of drip-feed micro aggressions. For instance, contributions from female board members being ignored and thus diminished. A trustee described a chair who seemingly "*Didn't like women, wouldn't listen to them, and only had them on the board to meet diversity requirements.*" We explore this type of issue further in *Chapter 6: Harnessing diversity*. There were other stories of bullies actively seeking to belittle their board colleagues by setting them up to look foolish or wrong-footing them. In one story, a fellow director reported repeatedly seeing the commercial director "*playing games*" with the CEO. He would produce the revenue figures too late for the board papers and then provide surprise updates in the meeting, in front of the non-executive directors. This made him appear more on top of the financials than the CEO. Another director told us about a domineering chair who gaslighted him – created a false narrative which made the director question his own grip on reality. The chair repeatedly distorted minutes of meetings by putting pressure on the company secretary to misrepresent key points. When challenged, the chair insisted that the director was being picky and had misunderstood or misremembered the conversation. As a new member of the board, the director lost confidence in his own recall of events and ability to understand them.

Many of our clients and interviewees have their own theories of why board members act like bullies. Some put it down to abrasive personalities and, as one interviewee noted "*Certain people have a very limited behavioural repertoire ... shouting and bullying and managing people in a very direct way.*" Others see it as a deep-seated need to show off, masking a lack of confidence due to underlying insecurity (one coach called it *"aggression insecurity."*) Initial research has suggested that bullying might be linked to some aspects of the big five personality traits, which we discussed in the executive/nonexecutive seesaw chapter. In particular bullies may be high in terms of neuroticism (with limited emotional stability), low on agreeableness (lacking kindliness and empathy) and not very conscientious (limited self-discipline and dutifulness) [25].

Beyond the normal range of personality traits, people can have personality disorders like psychopathy and narcissism which are associated with bullying. Psychopaths are generally highly intelligent, but are ruthless and impulsive, acting without fear and essentially amoral. Psychopathic leaders can be wily and manipulate unwitting colleagues, grooming them for their own means. Research over the last 50 years concludes that the personality disorder most commonly linked with extreme coercive behaviour is narcissism [25]. Outwardly this is characterised by a sense of entitlement, self-importance, grandiose thinking and lack of empathy. It's all about them. Yet in the case of narcissists, these characteristics mask a deep-seated feeling of inferiority and a profound inability to take criticism. For further exploration of these disorders, we recommend the classic academic work on narcissistic leaders *The Neurotic Organization* by Manfred Kets De Vries and Danny Miller [26], and Paul Babiak's popular leadership book *Snakes in Suits* [27], which examines the influence of psychopaths in business.

The victim

Studies confirm that being bullied can affect anyone – regardless of age, gender identity, ethnicity, experience or ability – and can take place in all sorts of work contexts. If it's low-grade bullying, then victims with positive personality types (who view the world as understandable and manageable and see their work as meaningful) may be more able to cope. As one interviewee said *"One person's brainstorm is another's sparring match."* In one instance, a coach observed a chair verbally *"beating up"* a CEO on a regular basis and raised this with the CEO, who responded that they knew this was the case, but said *"He's making me think a lot harder. Yes, it's too challenging, but I'm actually enjoying the experience."*

Nevertheless, if the bullying is severe, any personality type can feel the impact [25]. We and our interviewees have seen bullying arise from a power imbalance, where the perpetrator feels they can take advantage. Victims are often in minorities on the board such as female, ethnic minority or LGBTQ members, but it's not limited to these groups. The subjects of bullying reported a range of responses. At one end of the scale, a target described how the constant push back and sense of failing to get their point across felt *"uncomfortable"* and *"a little like bullying."* Also, there was a feeling of *"being a child"* again or" *going slightly mad."* At the other end, experiencing perpetual coercion resulted in physical or mental illness and wanting to avoid the workplace.

In our research, victims of bullying often reported a sense of disbelief that it could be happening to them and expressed doubt in themselves, as no one else seemed to react or notice. One female executive director who was subject to coercive behaviour by other women put it this way "*I'm an independent, grown, intelligent woman. How could this possibly be happening to me?*" She went on

> *When you're being bullied you start to internalise the fact that maybe I'm making this all up and this isn't really happening, because how can others not notice this?*

This questioning of yourself can lead to the belief that responsibility lies with you and you need to sort yourself out. Ideally, fellow board members would also notice the problem, and offer support by challenging the unacceptable behaviour of their colleagues. So why are targets of bullying left to fend for themselves?

The bystander

This leads us to consider the role of bystander board members, who don't intervene when they witness bullying behaviour. Interviewees commented that it can be "*Hard to challenge*" and "*It's not easy to tell someone who's in a position of power that you're not going to tolerate [their approach]*." Typical group bystander behaviour involves looking the other way and not questioning what is said or done. Social psychologists have explored this *bystander effect* – the tendency of observers of an incident or issue not to help if there are other bystanders present. In social experiments they concluded that such bystanders only act in limited circumstances: if they notice the incident, see it as an emergency and assume responsibility for helping [28].

Our research suggests that individuals on boards vary in their awareness of bullying and might struggle to work out when the situation is serious. When observers do intervene, interviewees admitted it was sometimes half-hearted. One board member confessed to trying to persuade the bully to become a better listener, despite being sceptical that they were capable of this. There were also illustrations of passive approaches and in these situations, bystanders seem initially to be malleable, wanting an easy life. Typically, nothing is said for some time and issues are left to simmer under the surface. Eventually emotions boil over and the board makes a move to confront the bully, which can be shocking for the perpetrator.

We also discovered a theme of fearing conflict or "*awkward situations*." As one interviewee reflected "*You never know how nuclear these situations can be.*"

*I just think boards like many organisations, are not particularly excited about
dealing with controversy and with tough situations as quickly as they should.*

A public enquiry into the collapse and subsequent nationalisation of the Royal
Bank of Scotland in 2009 identified this kind of avoidance. As early as 2003, under
CEO Fred Goodwin, there were concerns that board discussions often seemed "bullying in nature" and the atmosphere "often negative." The enquiry noted "The challenging management culture led by the CEO raised particular risks that had to be
addressed" [29]. Although the non-executive directors interviewed following the
collapse said they did question the executive, a Financial Services Authority investigation "was able to identify little significant disagreement on major issues … in
a board containing tough and experienced individuals." This was a large board of
seventeen directors. Why didn't they challenge the CEO's style and approach?

Observers told us about feeling alone and unsettled when they took a stand and
called out bullying behaviour. A trustee confronted a chair who, in his view, was
highly aggressive. The chair didn't think there was a problem, responding that others "*could always shout back*" and that wouldn't worry him as "*things don't stick
to me*." The rest of the board just stayed quiet, unwilling to break ranks. The trustee
describes how this typically played out: "*It would end up with just the two of us
sparring … I'm holding my punches, but I'm embarrassed to be doing it*." Table 3.2
is a summary of the responses of bystanders (or lack of them).

It's evident from our research that it can take significant personal strength and
courage to tackle bullying behaviour – to shift from being a bystander to intervening. This is particularly true in situations where the dynamic has become
entrenched over a long period, so that bullying has become normal. When this happens, people simply don't see it as out of the ordinary, let alone worth calling out.
Domineering behaviour can become an intrinsic part of the culture at all levels of
an organisation, from the board right down to customer-facing staff. In Part Two,
we take a closer look at how the boardroom environment can enable or exacerbate
undesirable behaviour.

Now let's draw on the perspectives of a bully, their victim and some bystanders,
to view an inside story in a professional services firm.

Table 3.2 Hallmarks of bystander behaviour

Is unaware of the dynamic.
Finds the situation hard to read.
Feels for the victim.
Fears confrontation.
Lacks belief that the dynamic can change.
Experiences awkwardness or isolation when they do intervene.

Inside story: In the firing line; your turn next

The management board of an international professional services firm was perceived by outsiders to be a tight knit group that was efficient at making decisions. The managing partner had been elected four years ago. She had previously had a hugely successful career, winning high-profile clients and building a global practice in a profitable niche. The remainder of the board consisted of partners who were heads of various practice areas and directors of the operational side of the business, including finance and human resources.

The managing partner had taken over at a difficult time for the firm, when profits were declining, and a fundamental strategy rethink was needed. She was a magnetic individual who made rousing speeches at partnership conferences and had very definite views. When she first took up the role, her style – direct and at times quite aggressive – enabled the board and the firm to take tough decisions. They were able to focus ruthlessly on repositioning themselves, profits per partner increased year on year, and the firm rose steadily in the industry rankings. Nevertheless, cracks eventually started to show in the managing partner's style of leadership. Profits at the firm flattened and in some practice areas they slid backwards. What was happening behind closed doors and what roles were members taking in the boardroom dynamic?

The bully's perspective

The managing partner believed she was being inclusive and collaborative and in meetings would often say that she *"didn't want to tread on anyone's toes."* She had clear ideas about the strategic direction that would best suit the firm and was determined that her tenure be a success. She worked long hours to achieve this, just as she'd done throughout her career. In return, of course, she expected the same loyalty from the rest of the senior management team.

This managing partner felt it necessary to robustly challenge other people's thinking. Given the downturn facing the firm, she saw it as her duty to set high expectations that would enable it to course-correct and thrive again. It was important to her to be surrounded by people of a similar calibre and approach. Sometimes she was deeply concerned that the directors on the board were just not up to the mark. To turn the firm's fortunes around, she believed they needed to display the same fast reactions, clarity of thought and willpower that she possessed. If they did not, she felt compelled to take decisive action for the good of the firm.

The victim's perspective

The managing partner was admired for her charismatic personality and tenacity, but when directors started to work closely with her, they realised how dictatorial her style was. She dominated conversations, never seeming to stop for breath. People making points or presentations were cut short. She also appeared fixated that certain departments were not working efficiently and would single out particular directors for hyper-critical treatment. Some directors described their staff, who had to present at board meetings, as being apprehensive for days in advance.

For several months it was the HR director's turn to be targeted with constant criticism. The board partners seemed not to notice, whilst other directors recoiled inwardly at their colleague's discomfort. Then, without warning, it was the IT director's turn to be scrutinised. For several months, he found himself subject to a constant drip, drip of negativity, as he grappled with a complex IT project. He suffered more and more restless nights and his home life was affected, with frequent family rows.

> *I couldn't quite believe how vulnerable and frightened I genuinely was. I felt like my mental health was being severely affected, because I was going home and not sleeping ... which was a horrible place to be.*

He couldn't understand why no one else on the board had commented or offered him support. "*You want someone to notice and to say how can I help or what can we do? If they don't, you start to think maybe I've overplayed all of this.*" He began doubting himself. It came to a head in one meeting when the managing partner made a snide comment about a minor issue staff had experienced after a difficult but successful software upgrade. The IT director thought "*Here we go again, the atmosphere is so negative and everything I say is wrong.*" He deliberately avoided eye contact, focusing all his energy on staring at his papers, just to avoid losing his temper and storming out of the room.

This time he was approached afterwards by his colleague, the HR director, who knew from personal experience what it was like to be the target of the managing partner's bullying behaviour. The HR director helped by taking the time to talk through – often, and in private – the problem he was experiencing. This was a welcome relief, and yet the HR director did nothing to support him in public. The IT director's frustration also grew with the other partners on the board, in particular the senior partner who had a pastoral role. Why didn't they see what was going on? Why didn't the senior partner intervene?

The bystander's perspective

Over the years, fellow members of the management board observed that the managing partner was becoming more and more controlling. The partners were busy in their own practice areas and juggling this with their firm-wide management roles. Although occasionally they wondered if they should say something, often the moment just passed, and anyway the firm was doing well. In the managing partner's appraisal, her behaviour was left unmentioned while other, more strategic points, were discussed.

Occasionally, during an informal drink after work, the senior partner tried to nudge the managing partner towards co-operating more with the rest of the board and moderating her style. Things would improve for a few weeks but then, under pressure, she would have an angry outburst. At the end of one meeting at which the IT director had borne the brunt of her frustrations, a small group of partners stayed behind after others had left. The managing partner observed that the IT director had seemed a bit agitated. The senior partner took a deep breath and mustered the courage to say

> *Well, I'm not surprised – I think he has done a great job on the upgrade, yet you focused on the one element which had gone badly. In his position I probably would have thought that was unfair and felt angry.*

There was an awkward pause, during which the senior partner calmly held the eye of the managing partner, while others averted their gaze.

The moment passed, but the managing partner was left with an uneasy feeling. To her credit, she dealt with this by calling the IT director at home that evening to try and clear the air. They agreed to talk things through outside the office the next day. That evening they both turned things over in their minds, replaying their own side of the story before they met in the early morning to walk together along a nearby canal. Were this pair's personal histories unconsciously influencing their relationship? We'll investigate some psychodynamic theories which seek to explain the mechanics of how this can happen, before re-joining them for their revealing conversation.

Psychological roots: From bystander to active intervention

In previous chapters, we've seen that psychodynamics is the branch of psychology that explores how our unconscious is often shaped by early childhood experiences. It also delves into the unconscious defence mechanisms we use to keep uncomfortable thoughts and feelings at bay. As a clue to what makes boards unwilling to challenge bullying behaviour, we revisit Bion's theories relating to unconscious behaviours in groups, which we first explored in Chapter 2. We also explore the field of transactional analysis, an illuminating set of ideas on ways in which our underlying patterns of feelings, experience and behaviour shape our communication. We examine what lies beneath the psychological positions of bullies, their victims, and the boardroom bystanders, and the nature of exchanges between them.

Depending on someone powerful

You'll recall that, according to Bion, groups in highly pressured environments can be unconsciously monopolised by dealing with the group's emotional state. He describes such prevailing cultures as their basic assumptions. When these grip a board, it diverts attention and effort away from tasks like governance, challenge, monitoring and strategic thinking. We've already explored the tendency of some boards to adopt basic assumption behaviours – like fight and flight or pairing – in standoff situations. These instinctive reactions, to the tensions of being in a group, might also be triggered by pressure from a bullying board member. Here we explore the third of Bion's basic assumptions, which is particularly relevant to bullies, victims and bystanders: dependency.

Dependency is the group's unconscious emotional need to be kept safe by someone or something that will provide for their needs [15]. It's the desire to be protected by a powerful leader or a god-like saviour, and Bion suggests it has roots in our childhood need for parents to look after us. Like children who need to be nurtured by parents to survive, perhaps board members unconsciously look for leaders with powerful and forceful traits, because they seem capable of ensuring the survival of the group and the wider organisation. For instance, board members might congregate around a leader who has a strong vision, clear direction and ability to innovate. The leader's aggressive drive brings the comfort of a seemingly safe way forward, which might explain the attractiveness of this type of leader. It might also explain why boards appoint and tolerate members with dominant and coercive characters, including psychopaths and narcissists, particularly in senior positions.

If a group feels dependent on a dominant, even bullying, individual, then it has a vested interest in supporting and enabling this person, and a natural reluctance to challenge them. But Bion also points out the other side of this emotional dynamic. Group members experiencing the emotional state of dependency also chafe against the feelings of inadequacy or frustration inherent in an adult searching for someone to look after them and take charge. This tension between wanting to be led by someone powerful, and resisting their leadership, may be strongly present in the boardroom. Groups in the grip of a dependency basic assumption are likely to place fantastic demands on the leader they have put on a pedestal to act as their protector and saviour. Since their emotional rock is only human, he or she is also likely to end up disappointing the group.

Whether it's a country, institution, organisation, sports team or board, the focal point of a group with the dependency basic assumption is the person perceived to be in charge, or an insurgent pretender to the crown. Actual and potential leaders are anxiously scrutinised and tested for their ability to protect the group. According to Bion's theory, a group reaches a tipping point when they can no longer ignore the fact that the leader is failing to protect them. Perhaps the emotional toll of bullying behaviour within the board, or reputational risk for the organisation, have reached intolerable levels. At this point members convey their disappointment and resentment by seeking out another potential leader to protect them.

The paradox of the dependency assumption is that when the dynamic shifts, the all-powerful leader suddenly becomes dispensable and can face swift rejection by the group. Usually, the group stays in the dependent basic assumption, simply switching allegiance to a new protector. This may be from within the group, or board members might look beyond for people, ideas, events or institutions that can save them. For example, in the RBS case discussed earlier, Fred Goodwin was finally forced to resign after the board was compelled to turn to the UK government to secure its existence via a financial bailout.

Bion's work explains how far boards may go in unconscious support of a powerful individual who seems to offer protection and preservation – and thus tolerate a bully. Bion's dependency basic assumption describes a general pattern of interaction that can arise within a group. We now turn from patterns of group dynamics to an area of psychodynamics which focuses on interactions between individuals.

Patterns of thoughts, feelings and behaviour: Ego states and life scripts

In the 1950s, Dr Eric Berne, an American psychoanalyst and group therapist, developed the theory and therapeutic practices he calls *transactional analysis*. This is a systematic approach to understanding people's relationships and communications. His ideas were popularised in his seminal book *Games People Play* [30], known by some as the first self-help book. Games are the unconscious way feelings from our childhood influence our pattern of conversations with others. As a pragmatist, Berne's aim was to develop a simple, accessible approach to understanding ourselves, which would apply to everyday life.

Berne built on Freud's idea of ego – the part of the psyche that mediates between our instincts, our conscience, and the real world around us, enabling pragmatic decisions about how to act. Berne identified that we communicate from three *ego states* – *Parent*, *Adult* and *Child*. These ego states are our patterns of feeling and thinking which are consistently associated with patterns of behaviour. We tend to be unaware of these linkages and how they form our personality at any given time. In the first and last state, we behave, feel and think as copied from parental figures or as we did as a child. We're driven by approaches and emotions from the past. In the second state, the Adult condition, we think, feel and behave in the present situation – the here and now – using all our adult rational capabilities [31].

Berne also believed that in childhood we develop a story about life – *life scripts* – with a beginning, middle and end. Without knowing it, we take decisions and actions which move us towards the final scene we have written, often unwittingly setting up problems for ourselves along the way. For example, in our inside story, the IT director's life script may tell him that however hard he tries, he will never be good enough. Using the language of transactional analysis, his basic position in life is that whilst others around him are OK, he himself is not OK. For Berne, everyone in an interaction would ideally take an Adult stance – one in which each person recognises others as equals, rather than feeling inferior or superior. He calls this comfortable and constructive position "*I'm OK and you're OK*." However, our life stories and scripts can get in the way because, unbeknown to us, they structure our day-to-day relations and shape our life. A similarity between a present-day situation and one from our childhood can trigger us to snap back into a salient Parent or Child ego state. For instance, when being criticised by an authority figure, we might respond by reproducing the thoughts, feelings, and actions we experienced as a child, when a parent was critical of our hard work. In the case of the IT director, this meant feeling upset and angry, and withdrawing from the exchange to protect himself from further humiliation and possible rejection.

The IT director's childlike response might well, in turn, trigger the parental ego states of his board colleagues, like the managing partner's critical parent script of finding and picking on faults. Her behaviour was founded in her life position of being OK while others were not OK (and the life story that she had to do everything by herself). In this way, board members can find that a rational discussion about an IT project becomes suffused with difficult feelings and emotionally driven reactions which are likely to have deep roots in individual personal histories. Particular combinations of Parent, Adult or Child ego states and scripts can combine in what Berne called a *game*. This is a pattern of interactions or transactions structured by predictable psychological rules.

Drama Triangle

Stephen Karpman [32] described one such game – the Drama Triangle – which can be particularly relevant to bullies on boards. He observed that whenever people play this psychological game, they come from the Parent or Child scripted ego states. They communicate from one of three roles within those states: *Persecutor, Rescuer* and *Victim* – as shown in Figure 3.1. Karpman defines these as inauthentic positions because they are shaped by the past, rather than responses to the actual situation from our current Adult position.

Karpman describes being caught in such a drama as "living in a fairy tale" with a "simplified view of the world with a minimum of dramatic characters" [32]. Usually, an individual has a favourite fairy tale and is drawn to stories and roles which fit their early experiences. At a given moment, our general stance, turn of phrase and the body language we use are good indications of the role we might

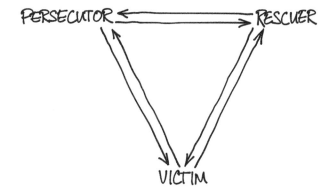

Figure 3.1 Karpman's Drama Triangle ©

be playing in an unfolding drama. They can give us clues as to how we might be drawing directly and unwittingly on life positions and scripts adopted in our early years. The intriguing thing about the Drama Triangle is that people switch around between roles. As events unfold, the Victim might switch to the Persecutor, attacking the Rescuer who becomes the new Victim. Within a heated board discussion, a director might find themselves cycling through all three positions and the associated feelings and reactions evoked by their role(s) in the drama.

We might characterise a bully on the board as a Persecutor. They aggressively criticise and humiliate a colleague, who takes the role of Victim being pushed around. So what's the bystander's role in this drama? The Rescuer position might sound positive and feel inviting, but each of the roles in a Drama Triangle has what Berne called a *discount*. An element of putting other players down in ways which minimise potential solutions to problems. Implicit in rescuing someone is the assumption that they need help and are incapable of fending for themselves. In our inside story, perhaps the HR director was drawn into the Rescuer role. She was dispensing help and support, but in ways which ignored the IT director's capacity to change his stance and be self-reliant.

This means that for bystanders witnessing a board colleague bullying someone else, it's important to resist the invitation to step into the Drama Triangle by taking up one of the roles, like Rescuer. Instead, they could build the capacity to notice their own ego states and the stories and scripts which may influence how they interact. This can help them make better, more Adult, choices about communication and behaviour in the moment. Berne encourages us to do this by thinking like a Martian – by becoming curious and looking at the dynamic in a neutral way, from a distance and without judgement. We'll look at some practical suggestions and techniques for introducing this change in the following *Advice* section. First let's return to our inside story, to find out whether the people involved were able to make sense of what might be going on, and take steps towards shifting this difficult dynamic.

Inside story: What happened next?

We re-join the IT director and managing partner as they walk along the tow path and talk. The managing partner set the scene, by saying that she was brought up short by the senior partner's feedback to her and had been reflecting on it. The IT director was surprised and heartened to hear her talk so openly about how the senior partner had intervened in such a straightforward way. The issue was now squarely on the table for them to consider together.

The IT director was apprehensive about discussing the issues. Being bold, he calmly and carefully described the patterns of behaviour he had seen on the board over time. He explained how frustrated he felt at what he perceived as unfair treatment and a lack of recognition for his work. The managing partner initially expressed disbelief, and then some embarrassment at her lack of awareness about the impact of her behaviour. After a moment, and biting back a defensive retort, she observed that when the firm was under pressure, and colleagues were starting to complain to her about things that were wrong, this triggered her feelings of inadequacy for the job. Her father had set incredibly high standards for her and her siblings, and she had worked hard all her life to live up to them. In a way, this drive was the secret to her success. When faced with evidence of not being good enough she would critique the situation, then push herself and others to do better.

On reflection she could see that she had not paid enough attention to the impact her approach had on the people around her. In a moment of disarming honesty, she acknowledged that she might in fact be more like her father than she cared to admit, and she committed to being more thoughtful about the impact of her behaviour on others. The IT director felt encouraged to acknowledge his contribution to the situation. He knew that he preferred to avoid conflict and not show his feelings in case others took advantage of him. This could make him hard to read and enable issues to build up a dangerous head of steam. The pair agreed to have a further one-to-one conversation in a month's time to see how things were going. The managing partner did not change her spots overnight. But this Adult conversation had expanded the range of conscious choices for their interactions with each other in the future.

Advice on banishing bullying

There was general consensus amongst our interviewees that it's important to address bullying issues firmly and swiftly. Otherwise, as one interviewee put it *"you're storing up trouble."* A highly experienced coach working in professional service firms makes a cricket analogy. A domineering partner on the board can be the star six-hitting batsman, but the rest of the partners are caught in a conundrum. They like notching up high scores and winning games, but can no longer tolerate the behaviour as nobody enjoys playing cricket anymore.

We've seen that there can be a range of underlying reasons for bullying behaviour. From enduring personality traits or disorders to temporary states, like when an individual or group struggle to find adult and rational ways to cope with perceived threats from others. Some factors are quite fixed, while others are more transitory. The key question for boards is whether the bully can change, or whether the dynamic is so ingrained and corrosive that they need to leave the board. How can you determine the best path and take productive steps along it?

First, we look at how to tune into the emotional dynamic on your board and use feedback to build awareness of problems and foster willingness to change. Then we share advice on how to proceed where people won't or can't change, and the board needs to call time on one of its members.

Awareness: Analysing your story

We've seen that humans have a habit of stringing events together in cause-and-effect stories. We do this to make sense of an ambiguous world and strengthen our sense of identity and purpose. But these tales, which are driven by conscious and unconscious beliefs and desires, can hem you in. They can limit your capacity to respond flexibly by adapting to the world around you. This means that the ability to notice your script, and potentially rewrite it, is a powerful tool. As a habit, it strengthens your ability to spot your own patterns and contribution to a difficult dynamic or unfolding drama. It also builds understanding of other perspectives and enables conscious choices to form better relationships.

To identify the story or script that you're holding onto in a bullying situation, try the exercise in Table 3.3, adapted from the work of Jennifer Garvey Berger [18], and Richard Boston and Karen Ellis [33], whose books we strongly recommend.

Looking back at your answers to these questions, what is revealed about your place in this drama? Can you find clues to your underlying motivations in your turn of phrase, your possible moves, your feelings as you review your answers? Perhaps some of the expressions sound childlike or parental and take you back in time to earlier days. Maybe you can find elements of Persecutor, Victim or Rescuer in some of your words or potential approaches, whilst others have a more Adult, realistic feel to them. It's also interesting to reflect on what you might be unconsciously seeking – what's really at stake for you? What psychological payoff are you after, and why do these things matter to you?

This type of reflection can widen your range of choice about potential courses of action and build your capacity to respond effectively around the board table. While it may primarily be the chair who manages board relationships, the onus

Table 3.3 What story are you telling yourself?

How do you make sense of the bullying board dynamic you are currently experiencing on your board? Think through and ideally write down some notes. Cast yourself in the best possible light and use these questions as a stimulus:

Who are the main characters and what are their defining characteristics?

For example: I'm trying to keep the peace; Alex ambitious and bullish; Sam thoughtful but passive; Amit creative but easily crushed.

What words and phrases come to mind in telling this story?

For example: I dread board meetings.

Alex is brilliant but acts like a spoilt kid who needs to be taught a lesson.

Amit won't put up with it much longer – he's going to leave us.

Why am I always the one who has to pick-up the pieces?

In very simple terms, what do you have to do in this situation? And why?

For example: Make Alex listen to people rather than shout and shut them down. It's dangerous for the organisation and I find the way he treats people disrespectful.

*What must you **not** do? And why?*

For example: Give in or give up. I feel it's my duty to protect the organisation and our employees.

What choices are there for my next move?

As quickly as possible, generate as many next moves as you can for your character in this story. They don't need to feel realistic or within the bounds of what you would normally do. When you've exhausted your creativity, add two more outlandish options.

Take some time to work through the list, seriously weighing up each option. Noticing how you feel about it, as well as what you think.

(Adapted from Garvey Berger, Johnston and ProQuest [18]; and Boston and Ellis [33])

is on individual board members to be alert to their own reactions to colleagues' behaviour and make conscious, courageous choices about how best to respond. As a former director of a large multinational puts it *"Whether it's a fifteen-strong board or a five-strong group … your actions should never, if you're honest with yourself, be motivated by fear or even shyness."* He sees this as an essential guard against being browbeaten, and above all else, counsels that it's important not to let your own fear of conflict hold you back from confronting bullying behaviour.

Crucial questions – Awareness

- What stories am I telling myself?
- How true are they of my current situation?
- What's really at stake for me here?

Relating: Choosing your stance

The same director observes that in his view, beneath the bluster, bullies are quite often frightened because *"they're bad at one-to-one relationships. They're actually afraid of confrontations*." His advice for bystanders is to grasp the nettle and make their feelings known to the bully in a calm and respectful way. For example, on one board a vice chair was extremely knowledgeable about the regulatory business and chaired the audit and other sub-committees. However, he was also very overbearing in the main board meetings. The chair recalled,

> *Occasionally because of his domineering personality, (the vice chair) would start to behave as though he were chairing the board. And I would immediately say with a smile, come on, I'm chairing this meeting, not you. And he would realise what he was doing and hold his hands up in horror and then apologise profusely afterwards.*

By consciously choosing to challenge in a gentle but direct way, the chair was able to alter the vice chair's stance. This meant that both could reach a less emotionally charged level of engagement. In this vein, and as an antidote to the Drama Triangle which we discussed above, psychologists and leadership specialists have suggested alternatives to the three drama roles. One of these is a different triangle outlined in TED* (*The Empowerment Dynamic) ® devised by David Emerald [34].

Power tool: *TED*(*The Empowerment Dynamic)®

At the heart of the TED* model is a commitment to conscious awareness of the role you are playing in a dramatic situation. You can use this awareness to take responsibility for your own words and actions, from a position of curiosity about what you can learn. This means mentally moving from the mindset that life is something that happens to you, or that you go along with, to a view that you can create your own life experience [34]. Moving from a drama to an empowerment dynamic involves choosing to swap a Drama Triangle role of Persecutor, Rescuer or Victim, with a TED* role of Challenger, Coach or Creator. This alternative lens (shown in Figure 3.2) can be useful in the midst of an interaction, and when working on a general tendency to be drawn into one of the Drama Triangle positions. Leadership development expert Jim Dethmer, an early adopter of the TED* framework, has expanded Emerald's work on ways in which you can choose these different, more empowered roles [35].

From Persecutor to Challenger

Dethmer suggests that the key to becoming a Challenger is detaching yourself from the beliefs and assumptions that keep you in the Persecutor role. This means questioning your judgements and asking how they are serving you and others in any given situation. It involves developing your ability to tolerate discomfort and the

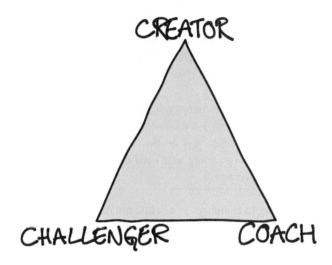

Figure 3.2 TED* (*The Empowerment Dynamic) ® (adapted from Emerald and Zajonc)

views that others may hold of you, and it particularly involves finding ways to come to terms with your own – and other people's – feelings of anger.

Challengers confront issues with compassion (to invite Victims to act) and they pay attention to the Victim's ability to receive this offer. They notice the person in Victim mode's capacity to receive feedback, and they stop giving it when it isn't met with receptiveness. You're in Challenger mode when you provide supportive pressure which encourages another person to take responsibility and play a creative role in resolving the situation.

From Victim to Creator

Moving from Victim to Creator involves taking responsibility by facing up to your feelings of fear, whilst holding on to the passion and vision which drives you. It's a shift from using your energy for drama, to using it to pursue your agenda with imagination. You can open up options for redirecting your attention and effort constructively by asking yourself questions such as: "If there were no obstacles in this situation, what would I be doing to create the future I want to see?" Like other moves away from Drama Triangle roles, it involves looking into your fears. These could be concerns about what might happen if you did accept full responsibility for the path ahead, or encourage others to take up ideas that you believe in. You're in Creator mode when you're inviting others to collaborate and explore possibilities for the future.

From Rescuer to Coach

If you've been worked with an executive coach, you'll know that they don't take responsibility for your issues or tell you what to do to fix them. They assume that you can resolve your own problems, and facilitate, question and encourage you as you find your own way. You can step out of the Rescuer role by taking this coaching approach. This involves putting your biases and agenda to one side and focusing on the person in Victim mode. In particular, it's about both of you looking at what that person can learn from the experience, and their potential power to take creative action. You know you're acting as a coach when you're really listening, encouraging someone to generate options and build on their thinking, inviting self-empowerment, and facilitating progress on their own terms.

Crucial questions – Relating

- What role am I currently playing in this situation?
- What role do I want to play?

Tactics: Changing the bully

Planning for succession

Good succession plans for boards are crucial, whatever the circumstances. They give you the space and security to evaluate analytically and calmly. A highly skilled chair of a multinational says that as soon as any CEO or chair steps into their role, they should think about who's coming next. In his view, this is because *"the legacy of what you hand on is the most important thing you can build."* That's why he's always at pains to promote proper succession plans. He debates them separately with the non-executives and the executives *"because it's, in my experience, the most difficult part of non-metric governance."* For example, in the USA, iconic Disney CEO Bob Iger made headlines when he left retirement (aged 71) and returned to the helm to address some of the mistakes made by his successor (whom Iger himself had chosen).

Planning for succession has heightened importance if a board wants to avoid tolerating excessively domineering characters – especially a bullying chair or CEO. Thinking back to Bion, such planning ensures that the board is not overly dependent on one individual, or prone to lurching towards another potential saviour figure, without assessing objectively their strengths and weaknesses. You need a plan B. Yet research by Stanford University and others [36] found that most large public and private companies surveyed couldn't immediately name a new candidate if a CEO abruptly decided to leave or was indisposed.

The main advantage of robust succession planning is that you can be proactive in anticipating problems and tackle them promptly. As a charity trustee who experienced a bullying issue observed *"The CEO was in danger of becoming, over dominant and abrasive and the board managed them out before it became a big problem,"* as they already had a highly rated successor waiting in the wings. The cultures of some organisations make this approach easier. For example, we notice that in the private equity sector it's standard practice to have active succession plans. Coupled with a tendency to be close to their businesses, this enables financial backers to spot early warning signs and stay in control of moving directors on.

With the security that good succession brings, how do you decide the most appropriate next steps in managing coercive behaviour?

Challenging to change

We've seen that better dynamics can be possible if bullies become aware of their behaviour and have the motivation and ability to change. One chair described using their annual board evaluation process, including structured peer feedback, as an opportunity to challenge a bullying colleague to alter their behaviour. This interviewee admitted to assuming initially that they would have to ask the coercive director to leave. The chair told this fellow director,

> *There's no point in me looking at all the other options because it involves you changing your behaviour and I don't think you can. I think this is just how you operate and it's not how I want to operate. And I don't think it's how we should.*

The chair instinctively took the role of Challenger outlined above, meeting her colleague's robust style with firmness of her own. She understood that laying down the gauntlet often appeals to this type of personality. In return, the director rebuked the chair for underestimating his ability to change and for being unfair. He was motivated to have a go and the chair believed that he was *"emotionally intelligent enough and definitely smart enough"* to think that there was another way. *"He was invested – he wanted it to work better than it was."* The chair recalls that, to the director's credit, they sat down and talked it through. He really took the feedback on board and made an effort to work in a different way. He had to moderate his behaviour and felt self-conscious, especially initially, but he did accommodate others, was less aggressive in board meetings and never swore at the chair again. This was well received by his colleagues and the chair was pleased with feedback suggesting that the situation *"was so much better."* The rest of the board were able to find their voices, meetings were much more productive, and these positive results helped the director sustain his new stance.

The key in this situation is that the perpetrator must want to change. As Henry Marsden, a leadership development specialist we interviewed put it

Fundamentally, it comes back to, they've got to want to do something about it. It's like the joke "how many psychologists does it take to change a light bulb? Only one, but the light bulb has to really want to change.

With some people there need to be a lot of negative consequences – losing their role, or job or income – before they make a change. "*There has to be the desire to make them want to work on something.*" This is particularly true if someone is in the late stage of a successful career, and coercive behaviour has become an effective strategy and lifelong habit. This brings us to the question of what to do when this ability or desire to change is completely lacking.

Building consensus

There will be cases where the domineering individual doesn't care about their impact or is pathologically wired to bully. Henry Marsden continues "*There are damaged people in the world, with no ethics or code*" who are dysfunctional. They may never change and are impervious to feedback and coaching. The challenge of working with such individuals is that

You're going to make them more charming and more able to get their way. And they'll learn things from you that will just make them better at what they are and not actually make a difference to the organisation.

So it's a good idea to be wary. And whilst our research found general agreement that it's important to give people a chance to change, boards can wait too long to exit members who are not performing well. It's particularly true when, as with bullying, the issue may be one of style rather than hard metrics. This is especially the case with removing coercive CEOs or chairs, where the politics and process can be treacherous to navigate and fears around disruption, succession and reputations impede action.

Building consensus for decisive action to remove a board member is easier said than done when the organisation appears successful by external measures. It can feel difficult for board members to stick their necks out when, for instance, the share price is going up and everyone's saying the board is doing a great job. But it's equally important to act in this situation. As a director noted, just because a business *seems* to be going well it doesn't mean that's actually the case. *"If you're worried about the dynamic or the culture, then actually you do need to pursue that"* as a director or a trustee. If you challenge behaviours in this kind of situation *"It's very easy for people to say you're overreacting … so you have to find a way to really surface those concerns and have them discussed."*

One board member noted that it often starts with one or two people realising, perhaps because they've had this kind of experience before, that the person is not going to work out. Then it may take time to get the other board members aligned.

> To be candid, the idea of having to find the new CEO is a really demanding, uncomfortable situation for board directors. Many boards don't want to come to an agreement about the need for change. Because of the work implications and the emotional implications of going through the process of finding somebody else.

Once several people on the board have begun to seriously question a colleague's position, the dynamics can become very unstable. What advice do our interviewees have for members facing this difficult situation? A senior independent director describes the careful and time-consuming process of testing out colleague's views, ever mindful of their allegiances and friendships. He describes taking soundings as *"Tunnelling through. Knowing we've got to stick to this and get it right."* He discovered a belief, amongst most of the non-executives on his board, that the CEO's behaviour was unacceptable. And he describes his next steps *"I spent an enormous amount of time in dialogue with people to try to work out whether there was really consensus as to what we needed to do."*

In this case he found that *"Some people got it, but didn't think it was worthwhile rocking the boat."* Others felt extremely passionate about the situation and thought that something had to be done immediately. He saw his job as trying to build a shared view about the way ahead. This can be a long process because, in his opinion *"You've got to take time for the views to percolate and form."* Ultimately, it's about working *"as grown-ups who trust each other"* and want the best for the institution. Through this type of approach, you can start to build an accurate picture and evaluate the facts from a range of perspectives.

Crucial questions – Tactics

- Does this person have the motivation and capability to change?
- Do we have consensus on managing this person out?
- How can we do it in a professional way?

Having a direct conversation

Once a board has reached a clear decision to manage out one of its members, it's time for a direct and respectful conversation. One lead director describes their approach to preparing for such a conversation with a coercive chair. In advance they noted down an outline of the things that were problematic about the chair's management style, and the negative implications for the management team. They wanted to be absolutely sure that the board's reasons were backed up by facts and circumstances that the board had actually witnessed. This director was then able to deliver the message clearly, calmly and sensitively. Using examples, they pointed out to the chair that he kept saying he wanted to include all the other members of the board in the discussions. "*But the fact of the matter is, in almost every case, you just dominated every single topic. And you berated the management team, which is not appropriate.*" The director then clearly explained that the board had lost confidence in this chair and therefore expected him to step down. They responded calmly and carefully to the chair's emotional response, before firmly inviting a conversation about the best timing and communications process for this exit.

This example shows the importance of thorough preparation, and of taking an Adult stance in the conversation. This lead director delivered feedback in a transparent and straight-forward way, and like the Coach mode in the power tool: TED* (*The Empowerment Dynamic)® gave the chair an opportunity to exercise some responsibility and creativity around his own leaving. Interviewees noted the importance of enabling the exiting board member to step down with dignity. In this case, they agreed that one of the most senior or long-serving members of the board would deliver the message. One who had "*seen this movie many times before*" and was able to approach it in a constructive and professional manner. Such status and conduct can be especially effective in managing people with psychopathic or narcissistic tendencies, who are likely to place great importance on these things.

Summary

Bullies, targets and bystanders

A bullying dynamic involves several elements: a bully, a target or victim of unwanted behaviour that makes them feel uncomfortable, and bystanders who witness the unpleasant interactions.

Identifying a bully

Boardroom bullies are often people with a combination of outward arrogance and inward insecurity. This leads to overt or covert aggression towards colleagues.

Anyone can be a victim of bullying, and it's the impact on the target which is important when evaluating the seriousness of a situation. Board members witnessing bullying may struggle to intervene. It takes emotional intelligence and courage to identify the problem and take steps to tackle it.

Psychological dependency and communication patterns

Groups under pressure can look to strong, heroic figures to save them. Boards may unconsciously feel dependent on the bully for protection and even survival. This can hold them back from tackling the dynamic. Models from transactional analysis suggest that present-day interactions are shaped by scripts and stories formed through early experience and games that people play. Games can fall into patterns of responses, like the Drama Triangle with roles of Persecutor, Rescuer and Victim, which is a classic bullying dynamic.

Awareness: Analyse your story

Explore and question the stories you are telling yourself and the positions you are holding, to help you understand your own and other's behaviour.

Relating: Choose your stance

Finding ways for all parties to take some responsibility for their role and actions can help resolve bullying situations.

Tactics: Confront the bully

A blend of raising the bully's awareness of their coercive, belittling behaviour through feedback, and challenging them to change, can lead to new ways of relating. When a bully is not open to change, the board needs to manage them out. Succession plans give you more scope to address bullying behaviour. Careful conversations are key to managing this difficult process.

Power tool: *TED* (*The Empowerment Dynamic) ®

Consciously choosing to move from Drama Triangle positions to alternative roles, in which you empower each other and focus on creative collaboration.

Further reading

Games People Play: The Psychology of Human Relationships by Eric Berne.
You Will Meet a Tall, Dark Stranger: Executive Coaching Challenges by Manfred Kets de Vries.

TA Today: A New Introduction to Transactional Analysis by Ian Stewart and Vann Joines.
A Game Free Life: The New Transactional Analysis of Intimacy, Openness and Happiness by Stephen B. Karpman M.D.

Part Two

Cognitive behavioural psychology

Mindset

How does the way you think about your environment affect board relationships? In Part One we looked at boardroom relationships from a psychodynamic perspective, in particular the impact of the unconscious and early life experiences on your present-day relationships. In this section we explore another school of psychology which can complement and expand your understanding of boardroom dynamics: cognitive behavioural theory. This focuses on the systematic study of the relationship between your thoughts, feelings and actions. We'll look at how your reactions are caused by events or triggers in your environment (behaviourism), and then consider ways in which your thoughts, beliefs and attitudes shape these responses and enable you to alter your environment (cognitive psychology).

Your environment shapes your behaviour

Behavioural psychologists at the beginning of the 19th century adopted the principles of experimental science, which posited that to study something productively, you had to observe it. So central figures like Pavlov, Watson, Thorndike and Skinner focused on analysing behaviour in response to different environmental stimuli. Rather than exploring a person's inner world and thoughts, they set out to "explain how the behaviour of a person as a physical system is related to the conditions under which the human species evolved and the conditions under which the individual lives" [37].

For example, a behaviourist seeking ways of minimising complacency on a board might make evidence-based recommendations about its composition, structure or processes, to help create a more pressured environment. Suggestions might include bringing an activist investor onto the board to expose it to critical shareholder feedback, create tension and drive change.

DOI: 10.4324/9780429340239-6

Your mindset shapes your behaviour

These early behaviourists took no interest in how personal histories, personality and characters might affect people's actions. They weren't denying the impact of our private mental experiences on how we act; they just believed it was impossible to study these in an objective way that could lead to reliable insights and predictions. Albert Bandura challenged this assumption, and his 1960s research led to significant emphasis also being placed on the way we think. His social cognitive theory included ways in which thoughts (as well as culture or environment) influence behaviour. Bandura's research examined the important interaction of personal factors, such as individual thoughts, beliefs and feelings, with our circumstances. And how we can manage our conscious choices to shape our environment (as well as their shaping us).

Engaging and asserting your board

In the first part of this book, we looked at the issues that arise from tussles for control, deeply divided opinions, and the coercive misuse of power. On these boards, people are caught up in difficult relationships, actively struggling to find sustainable ways to work together. The following two chapters investigate boards that have become passive, and lack the energy, inclination or awareness to voice their opinions. In the initial chapter on rubber stamp boards, we consider compliant boards on which, for various reasons, members have come to believe there is no point in being assertive. The subsequent chapter looks at boards which seem to exist in an ivory tower, where members are detached and distant from current reality or likely future developments. In many cases, they are just plain complacent. Cognitive behavioural psychology offers useful insights into the ways in which you can alter how you think, and change your response to the environment. This can enable compliant or complacent boards to re-engage and make an active contribution to outcomes.

Chapter 4

Activating the passive rubber stamp board

It feels like somebody's presented us with the perfectly crafted, beautifully sculpted crystal ball. You can see the inside ... but you've got nothing you can do to alter it. In the end, you sort of give in.

Trustee, academic institution

Introduction

One board member we interviewed recalled his first non-executive appointment on a charity board. He was excited to take this next step in his career while supporting an important global humanitarian mission. But his excitement cooled when he realised that major issues were being dealt with by a small group on the board and presented as "*a one-liner on a board agenda.*" It was clear that the conversation around the matter had already taken place. "*Beforehand, they were certainly agreeing that they had a plan of action,*" so there was precious little opportunity to engage in any substantial debate. He was receiving virtually nothing in the way of preparatory notes and papers. "*The board was definitely constituted in order to rubber stamp some stuff that had been agreed already.*" As a novice trustee, he was perplexed by his role – what did the organisation want from him? He reached the disconcerting conclusion that they wanted him to take part in a performance. "*This was a theatrical display for the donors, and any government scrutineers of what was going on.*"

Our experience and research suggest it's not uncommon for board members to hold responsibility for an organisation's conduct, whilst experiencing limited scope to act. Despite being legally accountable for governance and performance, they feel unable to influence decisions, challenge actions and ensure outcomes. Being on a board like this is a detached experience. The important alliances, crucial discussions, decisions that matter, are all happening somewhere – but not collectively at the board. This means that members are cut off from the information, processes and relationships they need to fulfil their responsibilities. The board is simply endorsing decisions that have been taken elsewhere.

DOI: 10.4324/9780429340239-7

These scenarios should not be confused with situations where the board appears to be inert but, behind the scenes, substantive debate and decisions are still being made collectively. In these cases, the board participates in full discussions of important topics, but this happens in private, outside of formal meetings. Usually there is collective agreement to this approach for a specific reason, such as commercial confidentiality. There can also be cultural reasons why board members feel unwilling and unable to challenge each other's views and opinions in the public forum of their board. A board advisor, with an academic specialism in cross-cultural business practices, noted the importance in some parts of the world, such as Japan and China, of "*saving face.*" This may preclude some open conversations at board level which other cultures would see as perfectly acceptable. In situations where societal norms discourage public disagreement, board members may still have influence. "*You're having all the same conversations, but you're just not having them in public.*" We explore such cultural differences further in *Chapter 6: Harnessing diversity.*

In truly rubber stamp boards, you don't have access to these behind-the-scenes discussions and this can leave you with feelings of helplessness – nothing you choose to do can make a difference. You feel powerless to perform your role. What can be done about this personally and professionally risky situation? In this chapter we explore how you might find yourself in this frustrating and exposed position, and ask what you can do to gain sufficient control to fulfil your responsibilities. We draw on ideas from cognitive behavioural psychology to shed light on the ways in which cues in your environment can shape your choices and actions. And we examine how you, as an individual board member, can manage your own thought processes and mindset to assert yourself on your board.

What are you noticing? The rubber stamp board

Let's look first at what our research tells us about the significant signs that you might be part of a rubber stamp board. In Part One we looked at the ways power is held on boards, and how it can shift between individual members and splinter groups. When a board has become a rubber stamp, power has been captured permanently by an individual or a group of decision-makers and is uncontested by others. Here are some dynamics that lead to the endorsement of decisions taken by others.

A sub-group holding sway

Power can be monopolised by a group within a compliant board. One governance advisor described a national charity with a very large board which was experiencing difficulties. Several members had been there for decades. She noticed that closed groups had "*coalesced around strong personalities,*" within which ideas and issues would be shared and discussed. When strategic issues were tabled at the board, the position of the largest group was presented as a block vote. They would effectively shut down other views and dictate the decision, rendering colleagues powerless. History, habits and the governance arrangements had set the scene for this problem. It was eventually resolved by significantly reducing the size of the board and limiting the length of service of its members.

It's also common for boards to split into groups along executive/non-executive lines, as we discussed in Chapter 1. A number of our interviewees described executive teams with a tight, sustained grip on board power. These controlling teams are often riding a wave of innovation or strong performance. Executive teams centred around founders or iconic CEOs, or which have turned an organisation around, were cited as potential engineers of unduly passive and compliant boards. They can come to be viewed as

> *magicians who have brought the organisation into a golden age ... and the board becomes sycophantic and that combines with a work force that is already sycophantic.*

These executives manage their boards by presenting issues, options and decisions in ways purposely designed to corral non-executive colleagues into a pre-determined position.

Power bases beyond your board

Our research also reveals boards which found their collective hands tied by a powerful group outside the board. One repeating scenario was experienced by regional or national boards of global organisations, which held full accountability for local performance, but felt controlled by the global board. A chair of a European arm of an international manufacturing company details his frustration. "*We would come up with some plan in Berlin where we had a very good team.*" This would be discussed by the European regional board who concluded that "*this is an excellent scheme. Let's do this. And then we'd have Indiana saying no, we don't want to do that. And why? Well, we're not ready for it.*" It was particularly galling as the European division was the most profitable, and yet was continually finding its decisions overturned. He concludes "*I might've been called chair of the European end, but I wasn't really in charge.*"

We've also seen evidence of the influence of power bases beyond the partnership board in professional services firms. A senior partner told us that if the managing partner wanted to get something through the board, such as the appointment of an equity partner or the opening of an office, they would come to the board with "*Well, I have gone around and meticulously spoken to every important equity partner and ensured that this has their approval.*" On boards like this, one or two senior people take on the time-consuming pre-preparation task of consulting influential figures at the firm beforehand. This means that when the moment of decision comes, they can draw on this borrowed power, so that fellow members have no choice but to fall in line.

Decision-making is a charade

In situations where power has been captured by a clique, or is held by external people or bodies, the board will go through the motions of its work without addressing the substance. The performance is a charade. Agendas are shaped, discussions held, decisions reached, activity and outcomes reviewed, but in a cursory way designed to signal compliance, rather than enable members to debate and add value. The non-executive member of the charity board we met at the beginning of this chapter expands on his experience where "*Not a lot was going on between board members.*" There was limited debate on controlled topics, but he surmised that "*All they were doing was airing a few topics just to make sure that the board minutes were robustly filled up.*" These could then be used by donors, particularly the government funders of the charity, who were scrutinising how the money was being spent. It was quite a sophisticated performance, where care was taken to demonstrate sufficient challenge, but really it was all an act "*expertly directed.*"

This type of behaviour can become deeply embedded, with long-term effects. One board advisor worked with high performing executive teams for whom "*presenting faits accomplis,*" withholding information or stage-managing debate, had become a pervasive part of the board's culture. For example, on a public sector board where a controlling chair had been replaced a few years back by a more competent figure, but still cast a long shadow. An executive reflects that his colleagues held onto an outdated belief that the board had a limited capacity to contribute. They continued with old habits of permitting their current board to only see "a *very pretty, well presented picture without ... enough information to prod and poke and scrutinise more.*"

Feeling helpless

We've described a range of characteristics of rubber stamp boards, relating to ways that power is held and decisions are taken. But what are the personal experiences and emotions of being on a board where you hold significant responsibilities, but feel severely constrained in your influence and capacity to act? Our interviewees described these situations as "*very unsatisfactory,*" "*uncomfortable*" and "*frustrating and irritating.*" One board coach poses an important question about board members who have responsibilities and no control. "*The rights and wrongs of why the decisions are being taken is one thing. But the other thing is, how are people*

Table 4.1 What are you noticing? The rubber stamp board

Pockets of power	The ability to influence is, in reality, held by a few board members; others are redundant.
Submission	Board members accept decisions as a done deal and see no point in debating matters further.
Overridden decisions	Board decisions are being quashed or changed by an external authority which has the power and the final say.
Anger and anxiety	Frustration, resentment and disbelief at your lack of control; anxiety about your accountabilities.

able to function under those circumstances?" She saw examples of board members showing signs of physical and mental distress and behaving out of character, as they attempted to find ways to manage their own discomfort. These included taking out their frustrations on people in their own teams, showing signs of feeling overwhelmed by their roles, and developing medical conditions. The psychological strain of trying to hold responsibilities, whilst experiencing little or no control, was making it difficult for these people to carry out their day-to-day activities, let alone function as an effective board. Table 4.1 summarises the various symptoms you may notice that indicate you're on a board where power is held elsewhere.

Being on a rubber stamp board leaves members feeling, at best, a little uncertain, under-utilised and devalued. At worst, it's a highly frustrating situation, fraught with risks that board members feel powerless to manage. This can leave them struggling to function and feeling trapped. Let's see how this type of power struggle can play out in our next inside story.

Inside story: Held back by head office

A board advisor observed an organisation's Australian board which felt obliged to implement decisions passed down from its European parent. Within this financial software business *"there was a lot of play of having discussions or getting different people involved in them,"* but this was just window dressing. In reality, the Australian board *"felt they didn't have any control as to what decisions were being made or that they were being paid lip service to."* Dictates were *"flooding down"* from the board of the parent company about which products to take to market and how. It was a one-way street. There were no channels for Australia to use their local market knowledge to shape the future roadmap for existing core global products, or drive innovation around new offers. This left the local board implementing strategies and tactics which they could clearly see were suboptimal in their markets, and chasing tough profit targets.

The situation was partly to do with the company's growth – scaling rapidly from its French roots into other territories. These new operations started as outposts from the centre, but swiftly developed critical mass. At the same time, applications for their technology diversified, taking varied forms in different countries. The global board had tried different ways of providing direction to this increasingly complex business. Over several decades the pendulum had swung from tight central command-and-control to entrepreneurial empowerment of regional boards. Following the recent entry of several strong new market competitors, the global board had returned to tight control, in an effort to transform the whole organisation.

Members of the Australian board were increasingly frustrated, feeling unable to use their experience and judgement to give direction to their business. And even worse, they were unable to express their discomfort. The previous Sydney-based CEO had decided to challenge a significant directive from the global board and been summarily replaced. The present CEO was clearly concerned that the same might happen to him and was "*squashing any pushback from within the Australian board or indeed any debate.*"

Board members described their meetings as farcical. They had directives about how to operate, they had targets and they knew that one would not enable the other. But any substantial discussion of this gap, or how to close it, was off limits. One member described the feeling of dread before meetings. Another talked about feelings of impotence afterwards, and how these would sometimes spill over into interactions with their team and even into their personal life. The board advisor was aware that several members were coping with the stress in quite dysfunctional ways, such as drinking heavily to numb their feelings. One member became seriously ill, and another realised that they needed to take time off (disguised as a sabbatical) to attend to their mental health. Unsurprisingly, the organisation's performance was slipping, and this board couldn't see how to reverse the trend.

What happened next?

The global board seemed largely unaware of these problems. The Australian board eventually began to change its fortunes when one member decided they could no longer tolerate the situation, and set out to build more constructive relationships with their global colleagues. She took the initiative to visit their offices and follow up with a series of virtual calls, to understand their thinking and share some of her own. This was a long, intricate process, but it ultimately nudged the pendulum back towards more local empowerment.

Later in this chapter, we look at how you, as board members, can change your mindset, improve relationships with power holders and assert yourself in decision-making. But first, we explore the psychology of how smart, competent people on boards can find themselves incapacitated.

Psychological roots: From learned helplessness to self-efficacy

Reward and punishment shape our behaviour

The famous experiments and accidental discovery, made by the Russian physiologist Ivan Pavlov, laid the foundations for studying how we respond automatically to triggers in our environment [38]. Researching the digestive system of dogs, Pavlov observed that they would drool simply on seeing the white lab coats worn by the people who fed them. They didn't need to see or smell the actual food. He realised they had become conditioned to doing this on seeing a piece of clothing because it had been repeatedly associated with their food. This is an example of how features of our environment can come to automatically trigger particular behaviours, although, like dogs salivating at lab coats, the response might serve no practical purpose.

Around the same time as Pavlov, other behavioural psychologists like Edward Thorndike were exploring another aspect of how we learn. His experimental findings led him to propose the *Law of Effect*. It states that "responses that produce a satisfying effect in a particular situation become more likely to occur again in that situation, and responses that produce a discomforting effect become less likely to occur again in that situation" [39]. This was taken further by BF Skinner, renowned for his work in the field of behavioural psychology. He investigated the way in which the consequences of our actions shape our behaviour and lead to learning. He experimented with rats and pigeons in so-called Skinner Boxes. In these highly controlled, enclosed environments, certain behaviours, such as pressing or pecking levers, were consistently followed by either pleasant experiences like food, or nasty ones including electric shocks. He demonstrated that it's possible to influence behaviour by manipulating the environment, rewarding desired behaviours and punishing undesirable ones [40]. This process is termed *conditioning* and leads to *reinforcement* of desired behaviours. Initially random behaviours can be targeted and trained in this way. Through repetition, even human subjects of conditioning become more likely to behave in ways which are rewarding and are deterred from behaviours which produce punishment or discomfort.

How does this apply to boards? Are boardroom environments rather like Skinner Boxes, with sets of incentives and punishments which, over time, reinforce or inhibit behaviour? On a rubber stamp board, maybe a passive approach has been easy and simple for members, particularly when nothing bad happens when they choose to go with the flow. If so, board members are incentivised to continue behaving in this way. And perhaps the people who do attempt to challenge or voice disagreement experience discouragement. In our inside story, the CEO had witnessed his predecessor being severely punished – by losing his job – resulting in damage to his professional reputation. The current CEO is thus highly motivated to behave in ways that avoid the same fate.

Learned helplessness

In the early 1960s, behavioural psychologists working with animals discovered a further feature of responses to unpleasant experiences. Their experiments involved studying threat conditioning and learning [40]. They gave dogs unpleasant electric shocks in situations from which they could not escape. To their surprise they found that when the shocks were repeated in situations where the dogs could get away from them, many still didn't make a move. Martin Seligman, now most famous as the founder of the positive psychology movement, termed this phenomenon *learned helplessness*. Passivity that results from prolonged exposure to unpleasant experiences which are beyond our control [41].

Seligman, a dog lover, gradually moved to studying this effect in humans. Using irritants as varied as loud noises and impossible anagrams, he found that similar patterns resulted. People who had been in situations where they couldn't get away or master these things, typically just sat there when next faced with these challenges. They didn't actively engage in finding ways of avoiding the unpleasant noise or solving the puzzles, even when this became possible. Afterwards experiment participants offered this insight into their mindset: nothing worked, so why bother trying? They had learnt to be helpless.

As well as people giving up on new tasks and avoiding exploration of new environments, Seligman realised there was another impact. People struggled to think clearly and quickly, and failed to pay attention "to the crucial cues that signal rewards or safety" [40] – a trait which is particularly worrying for boards. He dubbed the correlation between this helpless response, and the belief that actions will be futile, a *pessimistic explanatory style*. He noted that participants with this style frequently "blamed their failure to solve problems on their lack of ability and worthlessness." And he made one more striking observation: the hallmarks of learned helplessness are almost identical to the symptoms of a common form of depression. Perhaps this helps explain the mental health challenges sometimes experienced by board members facing these difficult dynamics, which we explore further in Chapter 7.

Learning the antidote: Self-efficacy

By pointing out the crucial role of a person's explanatory style, Seligman was making a major departure from his behavioural psychology colleagues. They saw human behaviour as predictable patterns of individual responses to environmental stimuli, conditioned over time. Along with a growing band of cognitive psychologists and psychiatrists, Seligman was convinced that how we think about our problems is a major determinant of whether we can relieve them or make them worse [40]. In other words, we are not limited to responding to our environments in predetermined ways. Changing beliefs, assumptions and mindset gives us the opportunity to examine and alter these things. This has been perceptively summed up as: "Between stimulus and response, there is a space. In that space lies our freedom and our power to choose our response" [42].

The psychologist Albert Bandura used the term *self-efficacy* to describe our ability to make conscious choices in pursuit of goals. In his view, our intentions are a key part of self-efficacy, since people are planners who set out to do things. Inspired by our motivations, these intentions give us a sense of purpose and a commitment to a particular direction of travel. (Even if they are partial, and even though we can't predict the future and are sometimes misguided.) Another important element of self-efficacy is forethought, as we look ahead to a desired goal and guide ourselves towards it through day-to-day choices. We can monitor our own actions against personal standards, reflect on how effective they are in moving us towards our goals, and correct our course if necessary.

Together, these aspects of self-efficacy give us the opportunity to exercise conscious choice in our lives. But cognitive psychologists such as Bandura and Seligman point out that self-efficacy has another element. We must believe that our behaviours and actions will make a difference. We need *efficacy beliefs*. Without these beliefs, we have no incentive to act. Bandura notes that

> It is partly on the basis of efficacy beliefs that people choose what challenges to undertake, how much effort to expend in the endeavour, how long to persevere in the face of obstacles and failures, and whether failures are motivating or demoralizing.
>
> [43]

There is also evidence that individual self-belief about worth and usefulness combine to form collective efficacy beliefs in teams and organisations. This research shows that the stronger the group's perceived collective value and effectiveness, the higher its aspirations and motivational investment will be. This means that group members have stronger staying power in the face of impediments and setbacks, and higher morale and resilience to stress. Together these things result in greater performance accomplishments [43]. But the rubber stamp board is stuck in the opposite position: lacking belief in its own power to change anything. It follows that to unlock the power of the whole board, individual members need to examine and challenge their own beliefs about their potential to act in ways which will lead to the outcomes they want.

You need to ask some tough questions about how you are explaining your current predicament to yourself and your board. Are you stuck in a pattern of learned helplessness in which the present uncomfortable situation seems inescapable? Are pessimistic explanations leading to passivity and dejection? If so, you can look for ways to shift this in favour of more optimistic, energising views which can lead to action. In the following *Advice* section we look at ways to achieve this.

Advice: On asserting a rubber stamp board

Awareness: Examining your thinking

Our interviewees agreed with the cognitive behavioural psychologists' view that people who find themselves captive on rubber stamp boards should step back and analyse their thoughts about the situation. They too advocate challenging beliefs and questioning assumptions of powerlessness. Simply examining how you are explaining the situation to yourself, and re-evaluating your range of possible options, can unlock your ability to take action and reclaim your power.

First, it's important to challenge your assumptions about your board role. As a serial non-executive director says, there is one question you must ask yourself as a non-executive on a rubber stamp board: *"Why would the organisation appoint me as an independent non-executive if it doesn't want my contribution?"* There might be a relatively simple answer to this. Perhaps the organisation likes the prestige or reassurance your name gives to stakeholders or is actually after your network of connections. This becomes a practical question for you about the level of personal resources you are comfortable lending to the organisation. There's also a deeper ethical question about your legal obligations as a board member, and the risks that you run in holding a largely ceremonial position. We recommend Ram Charan's book, *Boards that Deliver*, for an interesting examination of the risks of ceremonial boards and missed opportunities to drive organisational performance [44]. Reflection on these questions can inform a difficult decision, in line with your own values and ethics, about whether you choose to stay and influence or decide to move on.

Another possibility is that you might be a pawn in a power game, manipulated by those who are really in control of the organisation. People new to working at board level are particularly vulnerable to this and need to question the motivations of those withholding power from others. However alluring a pre-prepared solution proposed by the executive looks, it's essential to consider their reason for presenting it as a done deal. Is it arrogant resistance to advice, or is there a more sinister reason? For instance, are they really interested in having board members who just say yes and are easy to manage, to cover up unethical or illegal activities? As one board novice put it *"Perhaps I'm naïve, or maybe they hope I am?"* Potential pawns would also be wise to question their own motivations for holding their board position. If you are honest with yourself, perhaps you're complicit in the chess game and happy to relinquish power, because you are drawn to status and connections – or anything else you might find rewarding about being a board member.

Crucial questions – Awareness

- What am I assuming about my role on the board?
- What is the reason for the behaviour of others?
- What are my motivations for relinquishing power?

Having explored your motivations, a useful tool that can help you analyse your thoughts and take control of your behaviour is the ABCDE model, adapted from the psychologist Albert Ellis [45]. As described below, this is a practical way of overcoming assumptions of helplessness and achieving the self-efficacy beliefs that we discussed earlier.

Power tool: The ABCDE of changing your mind

We know from cognitive behavioural psychology that your perception of a problem, and your beliefs about your capacity to fix it, play a major part in whether you act positively to resolve it. Or in the words of the highly successful vehicle manufacturer Henry Ford "Whether you think you can, or you think you can't – you're right." So when you believe you're part of a rubber stamp board which has no real power or authority, your beliefs about your constrained ability to act can be part of the issue. They're also part of the solution. Because you can reflect on and alter your thoughts, which can change your feelings and enable you to take action.

The ABCDE process for doing this forms part of cognitive behavioural therapy. It involves exploring a scenario through structured self-questioning, focusing on:

A)   The facts of the *Adversity* you face.
B)   Your *Beliefs* about that situation.
C)   What you feel and do as *Consequences* of your beliefs.
D)   *Disputing* your own beliefs – challenging them and considering alternatives.
E)   Reflecting on how steps A to D have shifted your *Energy*.

Seligman, in his highly practical book *Learned Optimism* [40], describes and expands on this technique in work contexts. Table 4.2 sets out a simple worked example of what he calls a *wall-scaling exercise*, to help assert yourself on a rubber stamp board.

Table 4.2 The five-step ABCDE model applied to a rubber stamp board

Adversity

- Describe an example of when you were unable to assert yourself on a board.
- Include the who, what, when and where of the situation.
- Be specific, accurate, objective and factual.

I had just started to express my concerns about item 3 of the agenda when the chair cut me short and said that the matter had already been discussed thoroughly with the executive and they strongly advised adopting their recommendations.

Beliefs

- Capture what you were saying to yourself in that moment.
- What was running through your mind?
- Record it word for word.

"Not again!" "I want to say my piece"; "Everyone thinks I'm difficult"; "This is a stitch up, there's no point anyway"; "I don't think I'll even bother trying next time"; "Anyway everyone else seems satisfied."

Consequences

- Record the consequences of your beliefs.
- What did you feel and what did you do?
- Ask yourself: do your consequences make sense, given your beliefs?

I stopped speaking because I was frustrated – it all seemed futile and I missed the next few minutes because I was mulling over how pointless my board role is. I was reluctant to speak after that, so stayed silent.

Disputing

- Look for evidence that disproves your beliefs.
- Generate more accurate/optimistic alternative beliefs about the adversity.
- Put your beliefs into perspective.

The chair had shut several other people down too (evidence). Other board members are probably frustrated too and we can work together to improve things (accurate optimistic beliefs). I can find other opportunities to say my piece on that topic (perspective).

Energy

- Reflect on how your disputing changed your energy.
- What happened to your mood?
- What solutions did you see that you didn't see before?

I feel calmer about the situation, a bit more detached as if I'm taking it less personally. Next time I could say: "I'm noticing that we as a group don't debate issues as much as we might and wondered why that might be? I have a few additional thoughts and I would like to register my concerns before we take a final decision." How can I make that happen?

(Adapted from Ellis [45] and Seligman [40])

Relating: Letting go of board over-management

In our inside story, the Australian board has a set of assumptions about how they need to act in relation to the global board. They are managing the global board like a dictatorial boss whose needs and demands must be met without question. On the other side, those board members holding the power presume that the country-level board members have a limited capacity to contribute. As we described in the introduction to this chapter, sometimes these beliefs have been inherited from generations of previous board members. They endure, unchallenged, as part of the culture. And as behavioural psychologists suggest, defensive or evasive ways of behaving in response to this unpleasant stimulus can persist, long after a highly controlling non-executive chair or powerful outside stakeholder has moved on.

As a board advisor points out, this can result in powerful groups expending considerable time and effort on trying to render their board inert and ineffectual. This is sadly self-defeating. It's likely they would get much more value from building relationships with the other members and working out how to tap into the board as a resource. Her advice for rubber stamp board members who feel unable to contribute, is to table and discuss this openly between them. To have an explicit conversation about what the board is there to do, what individual members can contribute, and how they can improve decision-making, and ultimately performance, together. Shining the light of day on beliefs such as *"The board just ticks the boxes"* gives members an opportunity to collectively question their assumptions. To ask themselves whether they are missing a trick because there are other mindsets and behaviours which might serve them and their organisation better. Using the ABCDE model as a group can be helpful here, and there are other tactics for asserting a board's role in decision-making, which we cover next.

Crucial questions – Relating

- How can we build relationships to make full use of the skills, abilities, expertise and experience of the board for the good of the organisation?

Tactics: Fostering better decision-making

Right-size your board

We've seen from behavioural psychology that humans respond to stimuli in their environment. So changing the board environment – in terms of where, when and how discussions are held and decisions made – can enable board members to assert themselves more. Our interviewees favoured various ways to create more collaborative and inclusive decision-making cultures.

Board members in our research viewed board size as important. Unwieldy boards make it difficult for everyone to have a decent discussion and play an active role. A serial chair believes that you can't have complex discussions on boards with more than a dozen members. Beyond this you lose *"the real intimacy of the discussion"* and therefore don't get additional value. And there is a tendency for the real discussions to drift elsewhere and power to be held by a splinter group. In his classic book on productivity in teams, *Group Processes and Productivity* [46], Ian Steiner looks at studies in this area, to reach a conclusion. He found that groups are generally most productive when they have around 5–6 members, meaning that most boards are too large for optimum efficiency. Pushing to reduce the size of a large rubber stamp board may enable the resulting streamlined group to take the initiative collectively.

Taking decision control

The chair of a public company and a director of a professional services firm both advocate taking active control of decision-making processes to enable your board to assert itself more. Beyond standard governance about what level and type of decision comes to the board, they advocate making explicit agreements and plans to break up or *"chunk the decision-making process"* for important specific topics. This could mean tabling the topic initially for discussion at a high level – for example, establishing principles. Then board members have sight of it and gain an initial opportunity to familiarise themselves with the terrain.

Next the executive might consult with stakeholders inside and outside the board, taking care to use those discussions to test out and improve the plans. A non-executive has a tip for executive colleagues at this stage: avoid acting like a politician canvassing for votes – don't say *"I hope I can count on your support."* Instead, seek to really understand and address different perspectives, and demonstrate that you've done this. After this round of consultation, the topic is brought back to the board in more detail, perhaps this time for a decision. This may take a little longer. Nevertheless, agreements on this multi-stage process can help boards balance decision-making authority with the appropriate consultation of stakeholders. It means that

> *Issues are socialised, you've garnered views, there are no nasty surprises, and most importantly it doesn't feel like a stitch-up.*

Once you've asserted the board's decision-making role, a public sector non-executive advises frequent monitoring. In his experience, boards tend to move in cycles between too much and too little control. In his words, one month a board was rubber stamping at an "*abstract, concept level*," not fully contributing or making a real difference. Then "*18 months later ... it got back down into the weeds again*" so that the board became a log jam. He believes that boards need frequent reminders of their purpose and function – almost like an altimeter. "*This should be an annual contract to remind them that if you're looking at this sort of issue, you're far too deep. If you're only looking at this stuff, you're far too high. It's just getting the appropriate measure.*"

Saying something

In this and Chapter 3, we discussed the importance of speaking up and finding your voice. One interviewee remarked how rare it seems to be for people on boards to use their voice. He's been on several passive boards where something eventually went wrong, and it was only afterwards that board members acknowledged the problem. And yet he says of his colleagues

> You knew, you all went away and sniped about it. You went home and said "that was absolutely terrible and they're doing it again." But no one says anything.

A non-executive from a bank gives us a lesson from his experience on how to speak up. He comments that "*You can do as much due diligence as you want. But until you sit in the board and understand the dynamics, you don't know what it's really like.*" Once you've observed the compliant board in action, he advises first telling the chair that you're concerned with the lack of collective power of the whole board. This can be successful if your chair is listening to you and there are other board evaluation processes. Otherwise, it's important for you to discuss this with the other directors and, in particular, any senior independent director or other potential allies. You can then press the point together, as a group.

To help with this, it's useful to have positive examples of how things are done better elsewhere. One chair inherited a rubber stamp local government board that just routinely approved things. Rather than focusing on what wasn't working on the board, his approach was to look outside, see how others did it and ask if it was more effective. He ultimately looked to other regions for models which might reinvigorate the group. Similarly, board members talked about drawing on their own previous experiences of more assertive boards, to try and bring the same qualities to passive boards. This seemed to be particularly powerful when board members had experience of several sectors – which suggests that another shrewd tactic might be bringing in new blood, with experience on proactive boards.

Crucial questions – Tactics

- Is the board the right size for effective decision-making?
- What's the decision-making process for this issue?
- Where can I find support in raising my concerns about lack of influence?
- What examples of good practice can we provide?

Summary

Decisions are taken elsewhere

Boards can find that they are holding accountability for an organisation's conduct and performance, whilst experiencing limited scope to act. They are rubber stamping decisions taken elsewhere.

Your board's power has been captured

Sometimes power is seized by a group – a controlling clique – within the board. It can also be held outside, by global or higher boards or stakeholders with a strong power base in the organisation or sector.

It's a charade

Meetings become a sham. The board is going through the motions, rather than addressing the substance and members feel unable to exert influence. Holding responsibility with little control can be risky and stressful.

The impact of your environment and your thinking

Behavioural psychologists study the predictable ways humans respond to stimuli in their environment. They find that reward and punishment shape behaviour and we can learn a passive or helpless approach to unpleasant situations. In addition, cognitive psychologists emphasise the importance of assumptions, beliefs and mindset. We can choose to change these and develop belief in our own efficacy, to regain power over our environment, take action and assert ourselves.

Awareness: Examine your thinking

It's important to reflect on your beliefs and assumptions about a situation, and your own and others' intentions and underlying motivations. This can help you make conscious choices about how best to respond to a situation.

Relating: Stop managing the board and start using it

Individuals or groups who actively disempower their boards are missing out. The time and effort it takes to stage manage the board would be better spent developing relationships and working out how to tap into the talents of the board.

Tactics: Foster better decision-making

Review the size of your board. Large boards can make it difficult to have a meaningful discussion and take collective decisions. Explicit agreements about how decisions come to the board, and multi-stage processes, can lead to more inclusive decision-making. If you cannot exert influence on your board, it's important to speak up.

Power tool: Changing your mind through ABCDE

It can help to challenge your own mindset using the ABCDE process from cognitive behavioural therapy. This involves considering the A*dversity* that you face, surfacing your *Beliefs* and assumptions about it and their C*onsequences*. *Disputation* of your beliefs can then lead to *Energisation* of new options and possibilities.

Further reading

Learned Optimism: How to Change Your Mind and Your Life by Martin Seligman.
Boards That Deliver: Advancing Corporate Governance from Compliance to Competitive Advantage by Ram Charan.

Chapter 5

Descending the ivory tower

You just need to chip away and find out what's really the beating heart of the organisation, rather than being told that it's all great and looking at numbers.
Non-executive director, fast-moving consumer goods company

Introduction

Understanding what is really going on, in and around an organisation, is a testing task for any leader. An ivory tower existence – being detached from reality – is a particular risk for boards. As one of our interviewees in the construction industry mused, "*[on] a board it's always difficult. You don't know what you don't know.*" This may be because the organisation is complex and multi-layered, and the board is remote from its day-to-day operations. Or the board can be arranged in such a way that members' only contact with the organisation is infrequent board meetings. But distance can be just as much due to the way you think as to the board structure. You can assume things are going well because you take things at face value and lack curiosity to dig deeper. There may even be situations that you overlook, despite the fact they should be obvious to you. Our interviewee, the board advisor, entrepreneur and CEO Margaret Heffernan, puts this down to wilful blindness. In her excellent book on the topic, *Wilful Blindness: Why We Ignore the Obvious*, she describes this as "The small daily decisions that we make" to avert our eyes and remain "snugly inside our affirming thoughts and values" [47].

The fallout from choosing to overlook the obvious can be far-reaching. Take the food and drinks company Nestlé, which in the 1970s sold and promoted infant formula powder in the Global South, despite increasing evidence that it was unsuitable for use there. A public outcry and boycotts of Nestlé goods led to investigations, in which the company admitted failings. These included lack of research into users of the product in these countries, how it was being used, and the impact on infants, some of whom were malnourished as a result [48]. Half a century on, we see Meta (formerly Facebook) exposed, via leaks to the *Wall Street Journal*, as

DOI: 10.4324/9780429340239-8

being aware that Instagram is harmful to a sizable percentage of young users – and doing nothing to address this situation. Facebook's own researchers stated, in an internal document, that "32% of teen girls said that when they felt bad about their bodies, Instagram made them feel worse" [49]. This research was freely available within the company at a time when it was actively working on ways to extend the service to younger people.

These are extreme examples of organisations ignoring the needs of their users. A trustee of a charity likened this type of behaviour to a democratic government misunderstanding its electorate. In his view, "*It matters if you get out of touch with the communities in which you operate.*" When this happens, your organisation becomes distanced from its mission or purpose. Boards with no real concept of reality can damage the enterprise in the short and long term. Performance is likely to slide if the board can't see opportunities or get a grip of the root of problems. In the most extreme of circumstances, there is even the possibility of misconduct and fraud going unnoticed, leading to legal liability and reputational damage.

In contrast, successful boards are "*very good at getting a sense of the organisation itself.*" They invest time and energy to develop formal and informal systems to "*take the pulse of the organisation.*" Over time they amass a body of knowledge which allows them to assess the material being presented to the board. A key part of this is getting to know the people who underpin the culture of the organisation. This helps achieve the delicate balance of having sufficient information to be confident in what you are told, without needing to know everything. Such boards are also good at tuning into the environment within which the organisation operates and feeding back insights.

In this chapter we explore what behavioural and cognitive psychology can tell us about losing touch with your environment. In particular, how the biased ways in which you think can make you blind to issues, and how you can be lulled into complacency by watching the behaviour of others – even when they're poor role models. To counter these pitfalls, we set out strategies to help ivory tower boards put their fingers on the pulse. This is not with the intention of interfering with each other's roles, as in the power tussle described in the executive/non-executive see-saw chapter. It's with the genuine desire to understand what's really happening in an organisation and anticipate future challenges and opportunities.

What are you noticing? The ivory tower disconnect

What are the indicators that your board is disconnected from its own organisation, or the wider world of which it's a part? Below we suggest four classic signs, which may be subtle, and individually go unobserved. But viewed together, they show that beneath the surface, things may not be as healthy as they initially appear.

Looking backwards

Some boards have a habit of concentrating all their energy on analysing past data. They ask backward-looking rather than forward-thinking questions. Evaluation of this information is important. But is your board constantly assessing previous profit and loss accounts, quarterly financial figures, fundraising or projections of when financial backers can realise their investment? If so, this should be a warning sign. An obsession with rear-view mirror focus diverts attention away from looking at potential future risks – and opportunities. One governor in the educational sector, for instance, described their board as a relentless cycle of reading lengthy board papers on past performance. Emerging opportunities and risks were occasionally aired at infrequent meetings which created a *"lighthouse effect"* – light was shed on a topic briefly, but it was not monitored or revisited.

A reinforcing inward-looking bubble

Several interviewees also observed cycles of insular board behaviour. For example, where what goes on inside the organisation appears more interesting than scanning the horizon to understand what's happening elsewhere. Or when one internal issue, such as executive remuneration packages, monopolises board discussions. In this situation, a director in retail recalled trying to raise issues about what competitors or other providers were doing in this area, and *"getting blanks back."* They became concerned that this was due to the executives being out of touch themselves, because if the executives are *"in touch, they'll usually want to show you."* The director concluded that the management didn't have *"their ear to the ground"* and *"then you need to worry about the consequences."*

Another sign of potentially constrained information is when you receive data only via one source. Do senior management team's views all come through the CEO or are others allowed airtime? Do similar views keep re-emerging so that there is a constant loop of the same messages or stories? These situations can reinforce a particular angle, or spin on the data, which backs up a self-contained bubble of opinion.

Feeling complacent

One board member with extensive financial services experience observes that it's easy for some boards of high-performing organisations to be lulled into complacency. He recalls his early days on the board of a global multinational. *"I was always amazed at the board, those very, very important non-executive directors rarely said anything."* He asked a colleague about the lack of intervention. The colleague responded

Look, everything which comes to us has been so well thought through, mani-festly argued ... I just don't feel we are able to contribute very much. We're just impressed by what the board is doing currently.

But subsequent experience during the global financial crisis led this interviewee to caution that strong performance is no reason to abdicate your board responsi-bilities. In fact, the reverse is true. With the benefit of hindsight, he believes that board members should have been asking *"Why is it going so well now?"* Because this would have led them to a better understanding of the real fundamentals of the business.

Linked to this self-congratulatory style, we and our interviewees have also observed complacent boards painting an over-optimistic picture of invincibility. They have an unshakeable belief that their organisation will thrive, whatever the changes going on around them. In the last few decades, examples of this include Blackberry, the mobile phone manufacturer, who for too long believed that their MSM messaging service (and the need for a physical keyboard on phones), meant their product and market was impervious to the rise of touch-screen smart phones. In the media sector, traditional TV stations paid insufficient attention to the rise of digital media and streaming services, whilst Netflix had the foresight to pivot from being DVD-rental-only towards offering a pure online service. In the retail sector, some traditional retail shops, based primarily on a real estate model, proved out of touch with their customers' move online. These changes in customer behaviour were accelerated by the global Covid-19 pandemic, revealing complacent under-investment in online services and delivery infrastructure.

Avoiding bad news

Another telltale sign of boards being out of touch is when they steer clear of unfa-vourable information. In our work, we've seen this avoidance sometimes masked with platitudes and generalisations. On one not-for-profit board, everything was described as *"great"* or *"fantastic"* as they glided over topics. The chair let the CEO present the good news stories, without considering risks or potential problems. In another instance, executives in an SME were highly conscious that the CEO was keen to enter a new market, and so provided information that supported the narra-tive that the CEO wanted to hear. They were complicit in evading exploration of the downside. It was only with further investigation that the CEO realised this was only part of the story, and there were far more competitors in the potential market than she had anticipated.

In summary, Table 5.1 shows what you should be particularly aware of, to avoid your board becoming increasingly remote in an ivory tower.

Table 5.1 What are you noticing? The ivory tower disconnect

Backward focus	Board meetings are dominated by reviewing historical data and ignoring future trends.
Insular perspectives	Discussions concentrate on internal operations and viewpoints, rather than the wider context in which the organisation operates.
Over-optimism	Board members have a self-satisfied attitude, believing that current success is a sign that the organisation will thrive indefinitely.
Missing critique	Assessment of risk and analysis of challenges are glossed over and there's little in-depth questioning.

What happens when a board is oblivious to these warning signs? The following inside story illustrates what can happen when the board is not paying full attention to the realities of its situation.

Inside story: Blinded by the light

The trustees of a successful charity were proud of their global reach. Across Africa and Asia, they supported community health initiatives which changed people's lives. Over the last few years, they'd thrived and expanded their reach to cover South America, recruiting a charismatic CEO from a communications background to help raise their profile further. He was a suave networker who had brought in some high-net-worth donors whose funds enabled further expansion. A new trustee from a professional background had joined the board, keen to learn and fit in, as it was her first role at this level. During the board meetings which she attended in her initial year, she observed the positive picture that the CEO painted of the charity's "*magnificent*" achievements. He told moving and compelling stories from its programmes around the world, which gave trustees a feeling of pride in the organisation and its work. They felt little reason to question strategy or tactics when the charity was having such a great impact.

The chair was certainly knowledgeable, appearing to enjoy bearing most of the trustee workload. He said it gave him a "*sense of purpose*" and his colleagues seemed happy to leave the detailed exploration and analysis to him. The new trustee noticed that before and after the virtual board meetings there was little interaction between the executive senior management team and the trustees. Indeed, even at the lunch before face-to-face meetings, the trustees didn't seem to sit and talk to the executive team. The executives and trustees sat at different ends of the table talking in their groups, wasting the opportunity to discover more about the charity's operations and learn from each other.

After the annual awayday a few months into her term, the new trustee shared these observations with her fellow trustees over drinks in the bar. They reassured her that the chair would cover everything that they needed to know, as they could rely on his considerable charitable sector experience and good relations with the executive management team. You only had to look at the growth of the charity, and its increased number of community projects, as evidence of this. She asked if they ever talked to any of the country managers in the locations where they operated, as she would really like to hear directly about the good work they were doing. Again, her colleagues reassured her that they were quite comfortable that the CEO, through his well-established network of contacts, could tell her what was happening if she really wanted to know more. In truth, she was relieved to hear this as she was short of time, grappling with a heavy workload in her day job. She was also contemplating taking on a second non-executive role, as part of her plans for a portfolio career in a few years' time. She could therefore devote what spare time she had to securing her next role.

Out of the blue one evening she received a call from the chair wanting to pick her brains, given her professional human resources background and her safeguarding role on the board. He'd just received a call from one of the country managers, the level below the senior management team. The employee had said, "*You've got to do something. It's just disastrous – this place is a mess.*" Apparently, there were a series of allegations of sexual harassment and abusive behaviour by volunteer charity workers towards community service users on the ground in East Africa. He'd heard reports from other managers of similar behaviour in their countries too. The whistle blower said they'd tried to raise this problem with the CEO on a number of occasions, but he'd brushed them off and didn't seem interested. Now one thing was certain: the new trustee could see that she and her colleagues needed to turn their full attention to this significant problem.

What happened next?

After chatting with the chair, the new trustee saw that insufficient vetting of volunteers had caused a clear risk to beneficiaries of the charity. There was also the prospect of reputational damage to the charity if the scandal became public. She asked her professional contacts for advice on how they kept abreast of reality in their voluntary sector board roles. They shared their experience of good practice in drilling down to see what's happening on the ground in organisations and how to support, as well as challenge, the executive on this.

She then worked with the vice chair to persuade the chair, who was shaken by the experience, to adopt a new structure on the board. Now each trustee had a discreet geographic area that they were responsible for overseeing. The three of them made sure that the trustees "*had direct access to the guys running*" the in-country operations "*to make sure they never got into that position again.*" With the support of a shocked remainder of the board, they agreed a plan of virtual calls with country managers and field workers, to hear first-hand how their experience supported or differed from the information received in the board papers. The CEO ably managed the media interest in the story, but during his appraisal the board agreed a programme of coaching and mentoring in the weaker areas of his leadership.

The new trustee and her colleagues also learnt a salutary lesson. Never take things at face value; instead look for further corroborating evidence and persist in asking probing questions. Reflect properly and be curious about everything, instead of being blinded by the bright light of charismatic, seemingly competent leaders.

Psychological roots: Distorting and distancing from reality

In Chapter 4 we looked at how rewards and punishments from our environment shape our behaviour, and how examining our thinking and managing our mindset can enable us to assert ourselves. In this section we explore three perspectives on the psychological reasons why ivory tower boards might be out of touch with their environment and stakeholders. First, how biases in our thinking can lead us (and our board colleagues) to acquire a distorted view of an organisation's reality. Next, how a board might put distance between itself and the real-world consequences of its decisions. And third, how this cognitive distortion and moral disengagement can be reinforced and perpetuated by board culture.

Biases in our thinking

The work of several Nobel Prize winners illuminates how board decision-making can become divorced from the realities we face. Research by the cognitive psychologist Daniel Kahneman, and the behavioural economist Richard Thaler, provides clues to the irrational ways humans think and make decisions. They describe two ways in which we generally think. Our Automatic System, which kicks in quickly and finds fast and easy ways of dealing with issues, and our Reflective System, which we discuss in the *Advice* section further down in this chapter [50, 51].

The Automatic System is intuitive, unconscious and good at linking ideas – making immediate and efficient assessments of situations without much thinking through or investigation. It uses simplified intuitive thinking shortcuts called *heuristics* to swiftly problem-solve and come up with a close enough solution. These are good for rapid, practical solutions, but they are not always accurate and are led by an emotional, rather than rational, response. Moreover, they are made up of *biases*, where our judgements are prejudiced in favour of a particular way of thinking. Behavioural economists, who study the effects of psychological, cultural and social factors on the economic decisions of individuals and institutions, have identified some common biases which influence people's values, reasoning and behaviour [52]. Here are three classic cognitive biases which might lead a board to be out of touch.

Bias 1: Being too optimistic

Probably the most important cognitive bias for boards is underestimating the barriers to achieving their goals. It's the tendency to believe, falsely, that we're in control and that things will go well and be successful – the *optimism bias*. As Kahneman astutely says in his compelling, research-based best seller *Thinking Fast and Slow*, "Most of us view the world as more benign than it really is" which "fosters optimistic overconfidence" [50]. We only have to look at the number of start-up companies that fail as unfortunate proof of this. People tend to have an inflated view of their own abilities and see the environment as simple to navigate. When we watch others in our field achieve success, we often overlook the part that good luck plays in the outcome. This can especially be the case in smaller organisations, or with entrepreneurs, where there may be fewer management checks and balances or decision-making procedures to support robust, data-based analysis [53]. People then tend to use a few obvious, easily obtainable facts to reconfirm their optimistic view – and this is where the next heuristic is significant.

Bias 2: Relying on easily available information

Another common aspect of automatic thinking is basing decisions primarily on recent examples that readily come to mind. This *availability bias* means that we are likely to think that the relevant examples we can swiftly recall are more representative of what's going on than is actually the case [52]. On a board where recent ventures have gone well, intuition tells us that future ventures will also prosper. The fact that an organisation has succeeded for years under the current CEO and chair, might bolster our belief that these are the right people for the next stage of the organisation's growth. As well as picking easily accessible information to confirm our optimism, our judgement may also be skewed by the assumption which Kahneman describes as "*what you see is all there is*." This means that when a board is faced with large amounts of complex data, members will tend to concentrate on the information directly in front of them, so that decision-making is easier.

Kahneman points out that

> you cannot help dealing with the limited information you have as if it were all there is to know. You build the best possible story from the information available to you, and if it is a good story, you believe it.

[50]

It's dangerous to use only a few snippets of data to develop a narrative that makes sense, as it relies on "our almost unlimited ability to ignore our ignorance." This tendency explains why boards may focus inwardly on the organisation's own vision, mission and capabilities. And why members might rely on personal expertise and recent, relevant experience, while paying too little attention to the wealth of data about the aims, resources and capabilities of other service providers or competitors or the needs of potential customers. This availability bias can be the root of complacency for an ivory tower board. It can mean a board fails to delve more deeply or actively to seek intelligence from broader sources and form a more realistic picture.

Bias 3: Favouring the status quo

A third bias which feeds into the ivory tower scenario is our general tendency to lean disproportionately towards the status quo: to maintain the current situation or to do nothing. It's easier and less tiring to go with the flow and avoid the risk of losing what you have [51]. This loss aversion "is a powerful conservative force that favors minimal changes from the status quo in the lives of both institutions and individuals" [50]. We're drawn to keeping things as they are and would rather forego the chance of gains in order to minimise our losses. For busy board members, like those in our inside story, this bias can have a strong pull. They're likely to be active people with a variety of business, professional and personal roles. If they take the easy route and don't challenge the status quo, they can juggle all their commitments in a way that's manageable and doesn't take up too much time and energy.

Over-optimism, excessive reliance on easily available information, and a preference for the status quo are all biases that can play their part in your board becoming complacent and distant from stakeholders. Another more malign way in which you can detach yourself mentally is by becoming out of touch with the moral consequences of your board's decisions.

Losing touch with your morals

In the introduction to Part Two we described Albert Bandura's concept of social cognitive theory and the link between the boardroom environment, members' attitudes and beliefs and their behaviour. Positive responses to specific behaviour in an environment encourage you to repeat that action, whilst discouraging or punishing feedback tends to deter you from doing something again. We also saw that your own ways of thinking affect your actions, so it's a cycle of inner and outer worlds feeding off each other. As Bandura saw it, people are not only products of their own environment, but producers as well. For example, your own views and values shape the arguments you put forward, so that your board's decisions will be underpinned by your value judgements about what matters. This influence confers on board members a responsibility for the impact that their personally held values or morals have on people affected by the board's decisions.

Here we look at two situations which might cause you to lose touch with this responsibility.

The first is when you're physically distant from the results of your actions (as we mentioned in the introduction to this chapter). Behavioural psychologists have demonstrated that you are more likely to help someone with whom you have close personal contact, and there's a greater chance you will avoid doing something harmful to them. "The farther removed individuals are from the end results, the weaker is the restraining power of the foreseeable destructive effects" [54]. If your board lacks direct contact with the ultimate users of services or products, or others impacted by your decisions, you can feel a reduced responsibility and find it easier to ignore the consequences. Like the executive in our inside story, you can more easily brush off signals that omissions in safe-guarding procedures are leading to suffering, when this is happening on another continent.

A second way you can become detached is by mentally creating some distance, when you feel that you have to act in a way that's inconsistent with your own standards and values. Bandura and his colleagues looked at ways in which people can shield themselves from the guilt or self-blame they might otherwise experience about the consequences of their decisions. They systematically studied research in industries whose practices or products have harmful health consequences. And they created a comprehensive framework to categorise how these businesses, and the people within them, mentally distanced themselves from the harmful results of their activities [55]. This type of distancing can create an ivory tower of what Bandura calls *moral disengagement* for your board. We present his classifications in the following Table 5.2 [56]. It's a useful checklist for spotting ways in which you and your board might detach from the ethical consequences of decisions.

Cognitive behavioural psychology also tells us that issues like moral disengagement can be compounded by the behaviour of your board colleagues, and we turn to this next.

Fitting into your environment

Early in his career Bandura looked at how we learn behaviours by watching and copying people around us. He found that learning from others, *observational learning*, has just as powerful an effect on how we act, as learning from our own experience. In his famous 1960s Bobo doll experiments, he discovered that children who observed adults attack a plastic inflatable doll would act aggressively when allowed to play with the doll themselves. Just seeing the behaviour was

Table 5.2 Are you using these tactics to avoid moral responsibility?

Moral justification
Using moral, social, and economic arguments to justify harmful products and practices; for example, claiming that worthy ends justify morally questionable means.

Euphemistic labelling
Using sanitising and convoluted language to make harmful products and practices personally and socially acceptable. Cloaking bad activities in innocuous language.

Advantageous comparison
Comparing or contrasting the harmful activity or product to other activities or products that make it appear benign, of little consequence or of less detrimental effect.

Displacement of responsibility
Absolving yourself of personal responsibility for any harm caused, by viewing your actions as ordered by others and keeping yourself intentionally uninformed about the impact.

Diffusion of responsibility
Reducing personal accountability for your contribution to harmful activities by group decision-making, so no one really feels personally responsible.

Denigrating critics and victims
Attributing disparaging qualities to victims of cruel conduct, or to scientists or regulators investigating it. For example, investing them with sinister motives.

Attribution of blame
Blaming those who suffer the harmful effects of the products and practices for bringing the harm on themselves by their behaviour, deficiencies or vulnerabilities.

Minimising, denying or distorting consequences
Diminishing, altering, discrediting or refusing to acknowledge the harm resulting from injurious action or products, to minimise triggers for self-censure.

(Adapted from White, Bandura and Bero [56])

sufficient to produce this result, with no need for reward or punishment incentives [57]. Leadership training often emphasises the importance of being a good role model to others, and Bandura's work shows us why, from a psychological perspective. We learn and develop from watching others and deciding which behaviour to copy. Of particular relevance to us are his findings which show that you're more likely to notice someone's behaviour – and decide to copy or *model* it – if the person is of similar status and power to you. When you see peer behaviours as a route to success, you model their approach, because you have the motivation to copy them.

People joining ivory tower boards are likely to take their social cues from those around them. They may well come to believe that they're more liable to succeed by being as complacent as their colleagues. Other research shows that if you see others being passive, you've a tendency to see a given situation as benign [28] You are likely to feel less personal responsibility to intervene because others are present, and if they are calm you tend to interpret ambiguous situations as non-urgent. This is part of the bystander effect we described in Chapter 3. On an ivory tower board, the lack of concern shown by others can lead a board member to interpret the situation as being less serious than if they were observing it alone. Complacency is catching.

Given human tendencies to distort reality and distance ourselves from it, what changes can you make, as a board member, to address the cognitive and environmental influences on your behaviour? How can you become more aware of this, alter your board's biased thinking patterns, and stay morally engaged with the organisation and its stakeholders?

Let's see what our advisors think you can do to avoid perpetuating a culture of complacency and ignorance. As Margaret Heffernan aptly puts it, "when we confront facts and fears, we achieve real power and unleash our capacity for change" [47].

Advice on descending the ivory tower

Awareness: Picking up on your fast but flawed thinking

Building awareness of the limitations inherent in your own rapid, intuitive thinking is essential. We mentioned previously that as well as an Automatic System of thinking, you also have a more thoughtful and rational option: your Reflective System [51]. Kahneman describes this as the mental system which is "a slower, more deliberate and effortful form of thinking" [50]. It's a more conscious and careful way of thinking that's activated when complex calculations and choices need to be made. Using this to stop and review the ways in which you are automatically thinking and reaching decisions can help you spot biases, assumptions and gaps in your knowledge and engagement. Reflective thinking takes time and energy, but it's well spent. Hannah Burd, a consultant who works at UK social purpose organisation Behavioural Insights Team, explains that it's about always assessing *"what assumptions are we making and what do we actually know?"*

In the last chapter we advised examining your thoughts. A further step is to notice patterns of bias or assumptions in your thinking. It's a good idea to continually reflect on these thought processes using simple questions. For example, where am I not paying full attention? Am I being swayed by over-optimism or lured by the status quo? Do I rely on easily available information to confirm my instincts, rather than seeking evidence to the contrary? It's also prudent to consider whether you are in the habit of looking for ways to justify decisions that feel morally uncomfortable, as well as staying conscious of how your own views and behaviours are shaped by those of other people.

Crucial questions – Awareness

- Which biases are influencing me and what are the plausible alternatives?

Relating: Connecting across the levels

Building relationships with staff can help you get closer to the realities of your organisation. For instance, when you speak to employees or functions outside the board, perhaps you notice them complaining that they're not being kept informed. Or there is a lot of attrition, including senior or long-standing people leaving in certain areas of the business. Non-executives, in particular, need to be sensitive to the indications of what one called these *"wobbles in the system."* They are pretty good signs of non-alignment and potential trouble down the line. These connections can help you to sense whether the things executives say really reflect widely held views. Or if their optimism is an example of *"Tipping over from pride in the business into arrogance and complacency."*

A highly experienced non-executive saw his contribution to the board as much more effective because of *"open leadership,"* allowing him to talk freely to other layers of the organisation. Developing such connections is key to hearing, first-hand, what's happening, rather than just having it relayed to you. An example of such transparent and confident leadership was shown by a CEO in the retail sector. A new board director thought they needed to understand their digital operations better, so the CEO put them in touch with the head of online customer experience across the business. The non-executive director noted that the CEO had enough confidence *"to let me wander off on my own and lift whatever rug I wanted."* However, the new director was always mindful of approaching their visits *"with a light touch and not digging around in an abrasive way"* – staying focused on understanding the realities of the business, rather than intervening in ways which might tip the executive/non-executive seesaw (see Chapter 1).

In-touch boards often have a planned, rolling schedule of presentations from managers within the organisation who provide deep internal perspectives. As well as building relationships, these briefings mean that board members can subsequently ask more informed, pertinent and penetrating questions. Presentations like this also have the added benefit of showing you where the talent lies, and spotlighting likely management successors. These contacts open the door to formal and informal meetings and virtual catchups beyond the board, and introduce you to other groups and key people in the organisation, enabling you to build a useful network.

Mentoring, or reverse mentoring relationships where a staff member mentors a board member, can help you become closer to your organisation. Virtual mentoring relationships are especially good for connecting with remote areas of a business. With all these relationships outside the board, our advisors note that it's important to be sensitive to confidentiality and recognise the potential impact of your attention on people. As one director in the engineering sector observes *"by looking at something you change it,"* (in other words, people are often on their best behaviour when they're under the spotlight.) Also, be aware that just by taking an interest you can find yourself being lobbied because you represent the board. So be careful to filter your observations through an understanding of local and individual agendas.

Crucial questions – Relating

- Who can I build relationships with to gain a different perspective on the organisation?

Tactics: Triangulating your data

Visiting sites

In addition to building a rapport with the management level below, there are other methods you can use to get under the skin of your organisation. Site visits enable you to acquire more depth of knowledge about operations. This allows you to cross-check what you're hearing via the board with information gathered from further down the hierarchy, in a process of vertical triangulation. Of course, site visits need to be part of any new board member induction. However, interviewees also spoke of programmes of regular formal or semi-formal board visits, such as trips to warehouses, specialist units at acute and community health trusts, or factories, to see board decisions in action. For charity board members, it's useful to meet service users to better understand the issues you are committed to changing.

One former CEO and chair recalled spending at least three days every month going out to visit branches or head office departments to see how they operated. Indeed, questions were asked if other directors didn't do the same. In another example, at a telecommunications company which wanted to concentrate on customer service, all the directors spent time at their call centres, working alongside staff on the phones in the early hours of the morning. They also attended office socials across the country to hear employees' views in an informal setting.

Allocating specific areas of responsibility

Our interviewees also recommend assigning designated roles to directors or trustees to oversee specific areas and keep the board in close touch (as in our inside story). For instance, appointing a board member to the particular role of workforce director, with authority to talk to staff or commission engagement surveys and report back. In addition to being part of committees such as remuneration, audit or finance, such board members are charged with understanding a particular area of the organisation in more detail. One director in a pharmaceutical company explains that this was a good way of using non-executive directors. *"Each of us on the board had certain issues we were asked to concentrate on and I looked out for health, safety and environment."* She would talk to the safety personnel and then report back with her views on what was working well and what could operate better. This helped the board avoid becoming complacent or over-optimistic about the real state of the organisation.

There are examples of this type of mechanism being used in the public sector too. In the UK, the National Governance Association, which promotes best practice in the board governance of state schools, promotes the use of Link Governors or Trustees for different areas. For example, teaching and learning, safeguarding and special educational needs, and staff well-being and development. These link roles are medium term and usually taken up by board members for a few years. Their remit is to be the link between the board and the school, to deepen their understanding of how the educational establishment operates, and the financial situation in each area. They can gather evidence to better challenge the information provided by the school, and support it to meet its strategic objectives. They can also explore external best practice in their link area – which we consider next.

Bringing the outside in

The other aspect of triangulation is ensuring that you have broad, outward-looking knowledge of the external environment in which your organisation operates. To spot future trends, it's important to have a feel for what's happening outside, what other organisations in your sector are doing, and how the sector's evolving. We call this horizontal triangulation and there are various ways of achieving it. In the private sector for instance, one approach is to include a review of competitors as a standing item on the board agenda, to better understand how you are doing, relative to your peer group. In the public sector, it was insightful for a non-executive of a hospital trust (where infection rates were unusually high over the winter), to visit other health care trusts to compare good practice. In their view, this was a helpful learning experience *"to get to the root of what will help me to do my job better."*

The use of good technical advisors or experts also supports getting an outside feel on issues. For example, an independent view can be provided by the regular use of good quality auditors, who can flag up operational issues with the help of diagnostics and comparative tools. The chair of one audit committee observed this triangulation of information from the auditors working well, in tandem with the internal finance function and scrutiny by the audit committee. Others described bringing in experts to present at board meetings on important topics, such as the impact of climate change or diversity issues. Experts can also supplement and update non-executive directors with industry-relevant knowledge, as can board members attending external events like conferences. This is particularly helpful for areas where the board's collective know how is weak, and for complex, fast-moving topics like digital tech or sustainability.

Holding a premortem

We've seen that the ability to identify the risks and obstacles to success is an important element of being a forward-looking and in-touch board. One way to achieve this, devised by the cognitive psychologist Gary Klein, is the *premortem* [58]. At the beginning of a decision-making process, your board imagines that you're looking back on the initiative after it has failed (or in other words "died" – hence the term premortem). All your worst fears have come true, and everyone at the board table takes a turn to suggest a reason for the failure, thus collating a multitude of wide-ranging possible causes from different perspectives. These are shared in an honest way and scrutinised for potential biased thinking. This allows you to surface and address potential pitfalls, for example a competitor targeting and monopolising the same market segment. The technique lessens the political and cultural barriers to naming unwelcome concerns, because you're being actively asked to contribute your opinions. At a premortem you can ask a variety of thought-provoking questions. What if a key board member, whose pet project this is, leaves? What if essential technology doesn't work, or a pandemic or war breaks out? Individuals each imagine the internal or external issues that might jeopardise the success of the venture. Using this process to encourage your board to focus on what *can* go badly wrong is a great antidote to complacency. It permits a reality check, without dampening enthusiasm for the new initiative.

Crucial questions – Tactics

- What other sources and techniques can I use to get a more rounded picture of the challenges and risks facing the organisation?

Power tool: Deep dive

Another tool which your board can use, when it needs up-close understanding of a particular issue, is the *deep dive* – a one-off, in-depth exploration of a specific area or topic. One of our interviewees described being charged by the board to explore why the amount of fundraising in the charity had suddenly dropped. He assembled a small team, including staff members and external experts, with a clear remit to fully grasp the issues. To do so they interviewed key organisation insiders, plus external stakeholders, including funders and partner organisations. The trustee returned to the board with feedback that morale was not good. (The charity had recently lost several major donors and senior managers were struggling to set direction on securing alternative sources of funding.) This is a good example of a deep dive approach. A key aspect is that the presence of a board member – selecting and sponsoring a topic for analysis – ensures there is impetus behind the review (which can be lacking from a bottom-up initiative). Jack Welch, the iconic CEO of General Electric, saw picking out an issue for a deep dive as one of his "favourite perks" as "you can throw the weight of your position behind it" [59].

There are various deep dive methods you can adopt. The approach we describe here is based on a tool for innovation and creativity developed by IDEO, a global innovation and design firm. The five-stage process is explained and illustrated by IDEO's general manager, Tom Kelley, in his book co-authored with Jonathan Littman, *The Art of Innovation* [60]. We have modified it here to illustrate how it can be used to help distant boards resolve a strategic challenge by connecting better with their environment and stakeholders. This approach is powerful because it goes beyond just diagnosing problems to include creating and refining solutions. Once your board has clearly formulated a problem statement setting out the issue, a member can commission a deep dive team to work through the following steps.

Step 1: Understand your people, markets and technology

Analyse your current situation, particularly your 'perceived constraints' and possible opportunities. Advances in automated data analytics make it much easier for businesses to process raw data and strategise accordingly. Classic strategic analysis models like SWOT, PESTLE or Three Horizons are also good for this [61,62]. The purpose is to deepen your understanding of the realities and restrictions of your situation, and open your minds as to what could be on the horizon.

Step 2: Observe people in real-life situations

See first-hand what's going on by observing and talking directly to customers, clients, service users, staff and other stakeholders. Cut out middle people or focus groups. It's essential to find out people's concerns, likes and dislikes and what they find difficult. Act like anthropologists, by noticing how they behave and trying to understand the reasons why. It's more important to concentrate on what they are doing and their real-life experience, rather than just listening to what they say (like the board members who visited the call centres). It's also important to reflect on possible unintended consequences of any strategy or approach adopted by the board. And keep observing the response of stakeholders, particularly those who are passionate about the topic.

Step 3: Visualise innovative concepts and stakeholders

Brainstorm the new reality, and what the world might look like for stakeholders, to instil creativity, challenge rules and embrace change. An essential element of this process is bringing the topic alive, for example using storyboards to illustrate the future with characters. Another important element is creating testable versions of your solution – enabling multi-disciplinary teams to build a range of simple prototypes (if you are visualising new products) or implementing pilot schemes (for services). Don't forget to reflect on barriers to adoption. What's likely to get in the way – for example traditions and cultural customs – and how could it deter people from using your products or services?

Step 4: Encourage evaluation and refining

Try out, evaluate and refine your solution, looking for improvements. Involve end-users, staff and especially sector outsiders to test your ideas. Expect the unexpected and don't assume that everything will go well. User feedback on likes, dislikes and general preferences can be used to improve further pilots. Be prepared to tweak, re-evaluate and even fail. Scan other industries or sectors for ideas that might improve your solution. This stage is about iterative improvement using real-world feedback from stakeholders to test and refine new approaches, products or services. This will build links between the different parts of your organisation, and between the organisation and stakeholders.

Step 5: Recommend a solution to the board

Finally, take the deep dive solution back to the board. Revisit the problem statement and take members through the perspectives which emerge during the process. Focus especially on your insights into stakeholders and their behaviour, the characteristics of the environment you are operating in, and the data from your iterative prototypes or pilots. Invite the board's reflections on the solution and recommendations, and their broader perceptions on the process.

Summary

Out of touch boards

It's important for boards to be in touch with what's happening in their organisation, markets and environment. Boards can become detached from reality and complacent, leading to the risk of overlooking warning signs that should be obvious.

Narrow perspectives

Boards that are isolated from what's really going on often concentrate solely on past data, reinforce insular opinions, avoid questions about performance and future trends, or avoid unfavourable news.

Distortion and distancing

Biases in your fast, automatic thinking system can distort decision-making. They can lead you to be unduly optimistic, put too much faith in easily available data to back up your thinking and favour the status quo. You may also disengage from the moral consequences of your board's decisions when you cannot see or experience their repercussions. When board colleagues are complacent, you might experience a false sense of security because others don't seem concerned.

Awareness: Pick up on your fast but flawed thinking

Reflect on how you are thinking and reaching decisions, to help you to spot biases, assumptions and gaps in your knowledge and engagement.

Relating: Connect across the levels

Build relationships with staff at various levels to help you understand what's happening in your organisation. Management presentations to the board and mentoring programmes can also enable connections. You can build on these to form networks and keep your finger on the pulse.

Tactics: Triangulate your data

Triangulating the information presented to you at board meetings with information from other sources will improve your discussions and decisions. Site visits, designating directors to understand specific areas, and bringing in experts and advisors are good ways to improve board knowledge. Conducting a premortem can help you identify problems and pitfalls before you encounter them.

Power tool: Deep dive

A deep dive is a detailed examination into a critical area as a one-off, time-limited intervention. It connects you with reality, maps possible future scenarios and grounds your decisions in the real-life experience of your ultimate customers or service users.

Further reading

Thinking Fast and Slow by Daniel Kahneman.
The Art of Innovation: Lessons in Creativity from IDEO, America's Leading Design Firm by Tom Kelley with Jonathan Littman.

Part Three

Neuroscience

Brain and body

Your nervous system affects your behaviour

If you asked board members what their brain is for, the majority might say "It's for thinking." Actually, the primary purpose of your brain and body's nervous system is survival – using your body's energy efficiently to stay alive. Understanding this can help us appreciate why we respond as we do when faced with unfamiliar situations and undue pressure. Your self-preservation reactions to something out of the ordinary, and perceived threats, are a combination of the cognitive, emotional and physiological – because your mind and body are intimately linked. In previous chapters, we've delved into the sometimes irrational and unconscious dynamics of boardroom relationships. Now we consider what we can learn about the physiological basis for these emotionally charged phenomena, by exploring recent findings in the fast-changing field of neuroscience. As the psychologist and neuroscientist Lisa Feldman Barrett comments in her fascinating book, *How Emotions are Made: The Secret Life of the Brain*, "A purely rational approach to … decision-making sounds compelling, and even noble, but … the brain's wiring doesn't divide passion from reason" [63].

Your brain and body connection

Neuropsychologists specialise in studying the complex relationship between your nervous system and your thoughts, emotions and behaviour. Elements of the nervous system include your brain, spinal cord, and motor and sensory nerves connecting your limbs and organs of your body. Advances in brain imaging techniques, which allow the non-invasive study of the makeup and function of the nervous system, have helped scientists begin to understand the physical basis of human cognition and feelings. Your nervous system consists of billions of cells – called *neurons* – that collect and process information and use electrical energy and chemicals to communicate with each other. They form neural pathways

DOI: 10.4324/9780429340239-9

throughout the body and send messages to and from your muscles. This signalling system passes information around your nervous system, increasing or decreasing activity in pathways in your body and clusters of neurons in specialised areas of your brain. Neuroscientists have described this as a process of spreading activation, in which the stimulation of cells in your network of neurons depends on the number and links with other neurons [64]. Because of this process, you can perceive the world around you, have thoughts and feelings, take action and – most importantly for board members – operate with conscious awareness of yourself and others.

Neuroplasticity: Your change agent

Your nervous system is unique, partly because of the structure and function you inherit through your genes, and partly because of *neuroplasticity*. This is your brain's ability to modify and adapt the structure and functions of its neural pathways in response to your experiences. Your brain is continually altered by your lived experiences because the way in which you think or act, in response to your environment, strengthens the connections of some neurons and weakens others. Consequently, we all have different mental machinery, depending on the lives we lead, which means we all take in sensory data and process it in different ways.

Yet as we saw in Part Two, consciousness enables you to choose new ways of thinking, acting, and responding to your own emotions and those of others. When you shift your thoughts and feelings, neuroplasticity enables you to change your neural pathways. In short, you can rewire your brain and alter your physical responses to perceived threats from other people or difficult situations. You can also stimulate another aspect of your nervous system which is vital to boardroom relationships: the chemical mechanisms designed to promote social bonding and group collaboration. Recent research has shown that some personality types might be more capable of this kind of change. People high in the traits of openness and extraversion are prone to greater neuroplasticity, perhaps because they tend to engage more with the people and ideas around them. But board members of all personality types can tune their nervous system to adjust towards healthy relationships [65].

In this last part of the book, we draw on neuroscience to explain why we react as we do to survive in two very different board situations. In the chapter on diversity, we show how life experiences wire your brain for in-built biases in your thinking. We see how your nervous system responds if you perceive people who differ from you as threatening, and what you can do to change this. In Chapter 7, we explore what happens when board members face extreme pressure – a doomsday scenario which endangers the very existence of their organisation. We look at how your brain and body respond in a crisis, both in the short term and over the long haul, and we use insights from neuroscience to consider how you can work at your best under intense stress.

Chapter 6

Harnessing diversity

A diversity of approaches and experiences will allow you to horizon scan more easily for risks, for opportunities and innovation, and those things help a board.

A government advisor

Introduction

In most democratic countries, boardroom diversity is increasingly viewed as a desirable goal. Governments legislate to outlaw discrimination, and in some cases establish targets or quotas, like those for board gender balance set by Australia, Belgium, Norway and France. Many organisations invest in initiatives to bring a broader range of characteristics, life paths, and expertise into their boardrooms, to reflect society and the contexts in which their organisations operate.

Our interviewees described instances of making this strategy work well. In one case, the backers of a newly formed venture had purposely gathered a group "*of very different people with very different skill sets*" to form their board. Because of their out-of-the-ordinary profiles, the board jokingly dubbed themselves a "*bunch of misfits.*" But their combination of skills and experience greatly complemented each other, and their respect for each other was even greater. As they grappled with the new business, they tapped into each other's knowledge, generated all manner of ideas, and had intense and wide-ranging discussions on key decisions. Their differences in perspective, and ability to collaborate, drove success and unlocked value as the organisation grew swiftly and profitably.

Board members told us about other approaches to diversity. One non-executive, who joined a housing association board, was looking for colleagues with different life paths who were likely to come at a problem from another angle. Factors like social class and age can be crucial here. For example, boards with members young enough to be digital natives, born or brought up in the digital era, can benefit from this perspective. As research from MIT Sloan and others suggests "Having board members who are digitally savvy is a new financial performance differentiator"

DOI: 10.4324/9780429340239-10

[66]. Interviewees also saw how bringing neurodiversity into their board, including people with conditions like ADHD, autism, dyslexia, dyspraxia, dyscalculia and dysgraphia, could enhance the quality of their debate and decisions. This is not surprising, as these conditions have a physiological basis in brain development and functioning. As we'll see later in this chapter, these differences can mean that neurodivergent board members see different aspects of a question or problem. They may also process data in alternative ways – for example, by spotting macro trends and patterns – and be more inclined to generate novel ideas and solutions.

Despite increasingly widespread recognition of the benefits of diversity, progress is still slow. For example, in their report *Hidden Truth 2022*, Women on Boards UK point out that 50% of UK companies below the top 350 in the FTSE All-Share still have no women in C-Suite positions, and 75% of boards are entirely white [67]. In our research, board members and their advisors also reflect this slow pace. They were unanimously committed to making strides in recruiting and working collaboratively with diverse colleagues. But board members on nominations committees described tough choices between candidates with much-needed experience or professional expertise, and those with under-represented characteristics, for example women or people of colour.

And for boards who manage to appoint a diverse membership, there is a further hurdle: the challenge of navigating many dimensions of difference to reach sensible collective decisions. This is the challenge of inclusion – how to invite and integrate the points of view of people from whom you differ. As one chair asks *"When you've got people who have different backgrounds, different professions, different directorial skills, have different ways of thinking about things – how do you harness that?"* Confronting these challenges openly in the boardroom can feel fraught, as characteristics of difference are loaded with significance for individual members, and fear of giving offence can be a barrier to discussion. Even writing this chapter, we notice the limiting effects of our heightened concerns about using appropriate language and avoiding inadvertently prejudicial statements. Meanwhile, ideas about what is or isn't acceptable are constantly changing. If you're reading this book a decade after its publication, some of our words will no doubt jar. We hope you accept this with our good intentions in mind.

In this chapter we look at some of the neuroscientific reasons why progress on diverse boards can be so slow, focusing on how our brain is wired to process information and the effects of our physiological survival-based responses to perceived threat. We examine the way our nervous system is predisposed to support boardroom biases and exclude, undermine, or dismiss diverse contributions which could broaden or deepen a board's capability. We share advice on how you can consciously rewire your brain's social circuitry in favour of the many dimensions of diversity. And how you can push back on bias to enhance your board's ability to understand and solve complex problems and anticipate the future, so that you can harness diversity to *"see around corners"* and make better decisions.

To start, here's what you might see when your board makeup is too uniform.

What are you noticing? Your board is too homogeneous

Your board is an echo chamber

One executive director from the insurance industry described the world of some boards as *"a kind of circular club of people who come up through particular routes."* This can be perpetuated by a lack of governance around recruitment. For example, the use of informal methods to find new members makes them more likely to be *"colleagues or friends"* from similar social circles. He characterises these boards as *"quite collusive"* because *"they lack diversity in thought, in capability."* In boards like these you may find members tend to think in the same ways, reinforce each other's views, and rarely have significant differences of opinion. These are classic symptoms of an echo chamber: a situation in which beliefs are amplified or reinforced by communication and repetition, inside a closed system which insulates members from alternative views. Like the ivory tower boards in Chapter 5, homogeneous boards have isolated themselves from different views that could stimulate and challenge their thinking.

Even if your board has been successful in recruiting apparently diverse members, are you finding they really bring different perspectives? One chair of a board appointments committee describes his board congratulating itself on recruiting a Black CEO. He talks about the relief of knowing that the board would look more diverse on stage at conferences and pictured in the annual report. But at the same time, he knew the new CEO was *"a middle-class man from INSEAD and McKinsey, just like all the others."* In his view, the board had ticked a racial diversity box, but missed the riskier opportunity to recruit someone whose cultural background, training and life experiences would bring a significantly different perspective.

Failure to recruit diverse members to a group constrains its combined ability to explore a topic or question. Matthew Syed, in his thought provoking book *Rebel Ideas: The Power of Diverse Thinking* describes it as the limitation of being clustered into one area of a *problem space* [68]. When members of your board have overlapping frames of reference, it's as if you're standing in the same place to view a problem or opportunity. You can't walk around the problem, see it from different viewpoints, or bring insights that might be obvious to people standing somewhere else. Low coverage of the problem space results in a limited and partial collective vantage point. Under these conditions, board members tend to reinforce each other's points of view and simply can't see into and beyond shared blind spots.

How can you sense this restricted view in your boardroom? Perhaps there's little in the way of fresh inputs or perspectives, and not much to disrupt your thought processes. Debate on boards like this is likely to run along predictable lines: you already know your own and others' positions, and these are quite static. Together you repeatedly look at issues and topics from the same angle, perhaps using a time-honoured process or structure. You and your colleagues rarely develop new ideas or change your minds on a central question through board level discussion. One non-executive director in biotech describes what's missing as

> That tension of thought and discussion that just allows a bit of oxygen to the debate, so that you come up with a better solution.

Ideas not action

Another repeated pattern from our research is a board talking a lot about how to improve diversity but failing to act. Board members whom we interviewed shared many good ideas about how to recruit and actively involve people with varied perspectives. But although they had discussed these ideas with colleagues, they seemed to stop short of taking responsibility for making them happen. Perhaps this is because many of their proposed solutions had a long-term payoff. For example, one chair advocated working to bolster girls' participation in science, technology, engineering and maths at school, to increase access to careers in accounting and operations (which might lead to board positions). The effects of this kind of initiative take a couple of decades to filter through and would deliver no tangible benefits during the tenure of current board members. It takes a progressive board, with a strong sense of social purpose, to prioritise this kind of work. If your board is serious about improving, it needs to move from having good long-range ideas to taking action that ensures future impact.

Token gestures

You might notice that when your board takes steps to bring in people who can open up the echo chamber, your efforts don't quite hit the mark. Perfunctory actions can backfire because they feel like token gestures. For example, the practice of having at least one candidate with under-represented characteristics on your board recruitment shortlist, can inadvertently disadvantage those whom it's intended to benefit. One behavioural insights specialist explains that, in a situation where there is one potential candidate who is not like the others "*The signalling of: 'this is tokenistic,' seems to be incredibly powerful.*" Decision-makers' attention is drawn to the candidate's difference, so that choosing them "*feels unusual, and so feels risky.*" You might assume that the odd-one-out is there to tick a diversity box, rather than being there on their own merits – thus diminishing your view of them. Researchers at the University of Colorado have studied this phenomenon. They found that when there was only one woman or candidate from a minority background in a pool of four finalists, their odds of being hired were statistically zero [69]. So it's important to pay close attention to any practice aimed at promoting diversity. Will it have the impact you intend?

You can also pick up useful signals about tokenism from potential candidates for positions on your board. A 2021 Harvard Business Review article on women on boards [70] described how a successful female candidate refused a position because those interviewing her seemed more interested in her gender than her expertise. She shared *"I can understand what it means to be a token person. I don't like that ... I said, 'If you think my only value is the fact that I'm a female, I can't add value to your board.'"* Our research chimed with this, with a female non-executive explaining why she avoids boards where she has formed the impression that her presence would be tokenistic.

I just don't want to deal with the board dynamic that's there once I'm in the room because of a quota...you're there, but you're not really there. You're not really being listened to and you're not really able to change things.

Failure to include some board members

People with under-represented characteristics at senior levels, who are considering whether they will be fully involved by the rest of the board, are attuned to the issue of inclusion. Our research suggests this is astute. Within some boards, even those that pride themselves on being diverse, decisions are still made from a strong central powerbase, rather than by the whole board. In these situations, factors like industry experience, professional or social standing, financial contribution or shareholding can strengthen the voice of some board members – to the exclusion of colleagues with different characteristics.

When boards do recruit people from diverse groups, they can unintentionally reinforce this lack of inclusion by insufficient on-boarding processes and poor subsequent communication. One senior independent director in manufacturing noted that in such cases, *"some very basic things don't happen [and] there is a belief that people will by some strange instinct know what they need to do."* For example, the induction programme might just be a very simple introduction to various departmental heads and their responsibilities to people and operations, rather than a process involving more explicit conversations about the way the board works and how to make effective contributions.

When members with minority characteristics don't understand how to fulfil their role, it's a sign that your board is struggling to make the most of these diverse perspectives. Our research found this is particularly likely to be an issue when people who are unaccustomed to operating at high levels in organisations join boards. For example, boards that include employee representatives, users of a public service or people with lived experience of the issue that is the mission of a charity or social enterprise. It can be tempting to see the struggling board member as the problem and take action to 'fix' them by trying to give them whatever skills and knowledge are lacking, rather than addressing other causes, like the attitudes of fellow members. For instance, a trustee with lived experience of poverty shared their experience on the board of a large debt management company. They described a CEO who "*consistently showed a failure to listen and an attitude of entitlement ... Every time I opened my mouth he rolled his eyes. There was no wanting to hear and to learn.*"

One board advisor describes this inability to take advantage of broad perspectives as a kind of impatience. He sees boards that are "*just tolerating diversity or working around it ... They're quick to judge.*" They're struggling to be curious and say "*Oh, that's really interesting. What might we get from that observation? From sitting in your chair, seeing the world from your eyes.*" This genuine interest in minority viewpoints is vital to ensure inclusion of a full range of perspectives, but it comes with pitfalls which are worth watching out for. One warning sign is boards only taking time to explore diverse perspectives on certain limited topics, with members pigeon-holed into areas relating to their experience and background. For example, employee board members only being invited to report their colleagues' views on specific issues, rather than contribute their opinions across the full range of board topics. Or women only being given centre stage on stereotypically female areas, like employee engagement and well-being. Table 6.1 summarises some warning signs that your board might be too homogenous.

Now we step inside a boardroom which is struggling to bridge cultural divides.

Table 6.1 What are you noticing? The homogenous board

People reinforcing each other's views	Board members are similar and tend to agree with each other – you rarely challenge or change each other's minds.
Going through the motions on diversity	Your board talks a good game but doesn't prioritise action that will make a difference.
Ineffectual positive action	Initiatives to improve your board's breadth of perspective feel tokenistic and lack impact.
Minority viewpoints on mute	People with non-mainstream insights are excluded from discussion, or their contributions are undervalued.

Inside story: Mind the gap

At a UK social enterprise which delivers outsourced public mental health services, the executive team were alarmed and confused by their recent board meeting. It was only the third since a Chinese private equity firm had acquired a significant stake in the enterprise, and several of its representatives had joined as non-executives. The deal was potentially transformational, unlocking capital to invest in a digital platform that could change the delivery of mental health services nationally. But the meeting of minds, which had happened during negotiations and due diligence, seemed hard to recreate around the boardroom table, as members tried to agree a strategy and milestones for implementation.

The chair had attributed initial struggles to understand each other to the language barrier, but as time went on, she realised the issue went much deeper. She could see that her new colleagues understood the UK executives' words but were making sense of them *"from within their schema."* Very different frames of reference about public services, the nature of commerce, how organisations operate and appropriate boardroom interactions, were making mutual understanding difficult. Concepts and phrases which the board had previously used as shorthand (to convey a complex set of information) now had the potential to open up a chasm of miscommunication.

Compounding these difficulties were different communication styles and expectations about how to interact with colleagues. The chair noticed that the UK executives became frustrated, took up more airtime and turned increasingly animated and assertive. Instead of noticing and exploring points of misunderstanding, long-standing board members were simply explaining their position more forcefully – a bit like raising your voice when someone doesn't understand what you're saying. This was causing the new non-executives to feel distanced from their colleagues and become withdrawn, often waiting for pauses (which sometimes did not come) to contribute to the debate. Tension was building and the chair sensed that all members were beginning to feel defensive and question the wisdom of the new set-up. Some decisions had become urgent and there was no prospect of consensus. The chair was tempted to employ her usual technique of bringing conflict to a head and thrashing it out, but she had a lurking feeling that this wouldn't heal the growing rift.

What happened next?

The chair recalled the saying that *"the problem with communication is the illusion that it's occurred."* She had a hunch that a variety of cultural differences were causing board members to fundamentally misinterpret each other. She realised that the board had assumed that everyone would be on the same page once the new investors had taken a stake in the enterprise, when in fact they had work to do to understand each other's aims, values and ways of working. Although time was pressing, the chair recognised that the board needed to retrace its steps. She called each board member to discuss the gulf in mutual understanding and proposed an extended board session to concentrate on bridging it. The facilitated session focused on what the new non-executives wanted from their investment and why, and an exploration of these aspirations within the context of the UK health and social care market. The facilitator encouraged the group to surface and investigate each other's underlying assumptions, and really drill into areas where it was hard to understand what a colleague had in mind.

In this way, simple misunderstandings were cleared up, especially where people were using the same vocabulary or concept to mean different things. And some fundamental differences were put on the table for strategic discussion and decision-making before the board moved to the action it had been trying to initiate. There was an animated discussion of how to balance the new investor's desire to learn about the range of available technologies, with the executive's intention to push ahead with a known system. This surfaced an underlying cultural tension between exploring the market and bringing an attractive offer to the UK market in time for an important commissioning cycle.

The board members also benefitted from an activity that involved making simple requests of each other, designed to help them open up about their different styles of working. For example, by saying to colleagues *"You can assist me to contribute to this group fully by ... explaining something only once in the group, unless asked to repeat it."* We explore similar techniques, which invite people to adapt to each other's needs, in the *Advice* section below. But first we look at the neuroscience of how demographic and other differences can cause misunderstanding and defensiveness, despite our best intentions.

Psychological roots: Biases and the threat of others

Our brains are wired for bias

According to neuroscience, our behaviour, including our boardroom interactions and decisions, are driven by our *wetware* – the structure and chemistry of the body's nervous system. As mentioned in the introduction to Part Three, this consists of billions of neurons that use electrical and chemical signals to communicate with other neurons and with the organs in your body. In 1949 Donald Hebb, a Canadian psychologist interested in the role of neurons in learning, suggested that the more signals are transmitted between two neurons, the stronger and quicker that neural connection becomes. Simply put, neurons that fire together, wire together [71]. Activated neurons receive more oxygenated blood flow, and advances in brain imaging techniques now enable us to monitor this. We can map levels of activation in a person's brain as they perform certain tasks or functions. The technique of functional magnetic resonance imaging (fMRI) confirms Hebb's hunch. The more we think about two related concepts together, for example strawberries and cream, the more easily one of these things will bring the other to mind in the future. This association has become wired into our brain.

As we progress through life, our unique experiences wire and shape our neural pathways, determining the ways in which we perceive and interact with the world around us. They influence what we pay attention to, the complex layers of meaning we assign to an object or a concept, and the thought patterns our brain uses to process information and reach conclusions. The neuroscientist Lisa Feldman Barrett elegantly explains this process as the "tuning and pruning" of neural pathways. Some of the neurons frequently fire together, bolstering or tuning their connections, leading to learning. Those that are used less often are pruned away, dying off and making way for more useful ones [72]. This explains why, for example, board members who live in different cultures, or are from distinct social groups or generations, can bring usefully divergent perspectives. And why there is huge scope for them to misunderstand each other. It's because they are taking in and making sense of information in varying ways, as their neurons are wired together differently.

The kind of learning that is encoded in tuned, well-connected neural pathways can lead to automatic processing – quick and efficient thoughts, actions or decisions requiring minimal cognitive effort, conscious control or concentration. The way in which our thoughts tend to run along well-worn tracks of neurons, forged through repeated experiences, is part of the neural basis of the Automatic Thinking system we described in Chapter 5. It enables us to take fast, energy-saving, intuitive shortcuts in thinking, but this speed and efficiency comes at a cost. Existing associations etched into our brain can give rise to stereotyped thinking, where we assume that all people or things, with a particular characteristic, are the same.

As O'Connor and Lages explain in their highly practical book, *Coaching the Brain: Practical Applications of Neuroscience to Coaching,*

> What we repeatedly think about gets easier to think. This is how we build thinking habits that empower us or keep us limited; the mental equivalents of our physical habits. The thoughts we entertain on a regular basis go from being our guests to our lodgers to, perhaps eventually, our masters.

> [73]

Such masters may explain why people who sincerely wish to harness diversity on their boards find themselves acting in ways which *exclude* people from whom they differ. For example, if most effective non-executives you've encountered in your career have been men, then you are likely to have formed strong neural associations between the concepts of masculinity and success in the role. These existing neural pathways build prejudice into the way you perceive and evaluate people, and are likely to lead to unconscious bias when you're engaged in activities like recruiting or deciding whose views to pay attention to in a board discussion.

Them and us: Triggering your physiological defences

Unconscious biases wired into our nervous system by experiences can interact with other aspects of our nervous system in ways that make it hard for us to behave inclusively. For example, our brain may harbour a bias against people from a different socio-economic group or racial heritage, so that their presence in the boardroom makes us uncomfortable. Neuroscientist Joseph LeDoux coined the term *survival circuits* for the neural mechanisms by which we respond to discomfort and perceived threats. His research and writing on this topic give centre stage to our amygdala – a pair of almond-shaped clusters of specialised brain cells, one on each side of our brain, behind our eyes. Together they play a direct role in detecting threats, and controlling subsequent physiological and behavioural responses, by activating parts of our nervous system. They also contribute indirectly to felt responses like fear and anxiety.

Our amygdala's quick-and-dirty scanning of inputs from our senses triggers lightning-fast reactions when it registers a perceived threat, and initiates the production of chemicals like neurotransmitters and hormones [74]. Neurotransmitters relay signals between neurons to either stimulate or calm the nerve cells. Hormones are secreted by glands into our bloodstream, from where they can be detected by receptive target cells in tissues or organs. The threat detection triggers a receptor specific change like an increase in heart rate or energy production. Threat responses like these are intended to ready us physically and psychologically to deal with the adversity we face, in order to survive [74]. These survival circuits work incredibly fast, below the level of awareness and independently of other brain functions. We've all had the experience of our nervous system triggering a defensive physical reaction of flinching from something burning us, before consciously registering that it's hot. In the same way, we might act on an instant defensive response – without thinking – when we perceive another individual as threatening. It's another example of swift, efficient automatic thinking, which can save us time and energy, but opens the door to prejudice because it's outside our conscious control.

How does this play out when we're working on a board with people who have a diverse range of characteristics and experiences? In their insightful book, *Neuroscience of Inclusion*, Mary Casey and Shannon Murphy Robinson use data from neuroscience experiments to demonstrate that, when we encounter people who aren't like us, our brain registers this difference as discomfort and threat [75]. They assert that evolution has shaped the nervous system for collaboration within a group, and competition outside of it. This means that we are predisposed to frame people we meet into an in-group and out-group, as friends or foes, and fall into the trap of *othering* – viewing out-group members as intrinsically different from, and even alien to, ourselves.

Split-second mental categorisations like this can trigger amygdala-based survival circuits and cause the release of hormones and neurotransmitters associated with stress, especially epinephrine, norepinephrine and cortisol. In turn this results in a narrowing of perceptual field to enable focus on the perceived threat. The prefrontal cortex, the frontal lobe of our brain which is key to decision-making, is constrained to preserve energy and concentrate on the potential threat to survival [76]. Unfortunately, this also diminishes our ability to take time to listen, see the world through the eyes of others, and move beyond preconceived ideas and assumptions.

The effect on behaviour may be small, but is easily perceived by the survival circuits of people we're interacting with. Everyone's amygdala is particularly sensitive to subtle social signals conveyed through facial expressions – sometimes known as *micro-messages*. Perhaps we make eye contact when greeting a board colleague from a different racial group for several seconds less than others. Our colleague's survival system automatically detects this difference and triggers physiological responses designed to protect them in a potentially hostile situation. On the surface, two board members are greeting each other as equals in a professional way, but our nervous systems are sending signals that set up a different dynamic. This is one example of the effects of our in-built 'us vs them' base instinct, which are subtle but pervasive. It's one of the many ways in which the response of our survival circuits – to people who are different – can affect brain chemistry and undermine conscious intentions to foster inclusivity in the boardroom.

Neuroplasticity and social circuitry

We've seen that the leaps our brains have learnt to take, to make responding to the world around us more manageable, can build in bias and lead to misunderstandings with people who are different from us. But we've also seen that our nervous system changes through our experiences. This neuroplasticity – the ability of the brain to change through the creation of new neurons and neural pathways – offers ways of improving our capacity to benefit from diverse perspectives. Through consciously choosing to surface and challenge our own biases, we can forge new inclusive neural connections to strengthen our *social circuitry* – aspects of our nervous system that enable connection and bonding with others.

Neuroscience tells us that to rewire our nervous system, four factors are necessary:

- The first is focused attention, because this is the mechanism by which the finite resources of the brain are trained on a particular stimulus or activity.
- Next is deliberate repetition of a thought or mental practice – for example, listing the benefits arising from diverse perspectives after a board meeting. This reinforces it in our brain, strengthening neural associations, making us more likely to think this way in the future, and possibly making it an automatic habit.
- Both focused attention and repetition require the third element, which is motivated willpower to make a change. Becoming clear about why we believe it is important to make a change and setting ourselves a challenge can help. This is because we engage the reward mechanisms in our brain that release *dopamine*, the neurotransmitter associated with alertness, learning and a 'can do' attitude [77].
- The final ingredient is a conducive environment – one in which we feel supported by colleagues and sufficiently safe to focus on making a change [75]. Psychologically safe environments, like those described in Chapter 1, give survival circuits a rest from threat, minimising defensive reactions and setting the scene for clear thinking and collaboration.

Making a list of the benefits of diverse perspectives is an example of an appreciative practice. Recent studies show that this type of appreciation-based technique has "a positive impact on both the micro-messages in the work environment and also supports the brain in establishing new unconscious patterns, norms, and assumptions that promote inclusive attitudes and behaviours" [75]. As we've seen in previous chapters, we can choose to generate positive feelings, such as appreciation, and this has been shown to improve empathy and compassion in ourselves and others too. It's catching.

You can use attitudes like appreciation to trigger an upward spiral of open and inclusive thoughts and feelings based on your biochemical responses as a board member. There is good evidence that positive feelings like these stabilise your prefrontal cortex – the part of your brain that can consider others' perspectives and needs, detect and consciously override biases and habits, and actively choose attitudes like empathy. Helpfully for board tasks, it also enables focus, concentration, cognitive flexibility and creativity and the processing of information.

The main neural basis of this is the production of the hormone oxytocin, which we release when we feel loved and appreciated. This brain chemical, sometimes known as the attachment hormone, promotes bonding and trust between people. Crucially for harnessing diversity "it is also instrumental in the brain's ability to shift from self-interest to seeing others' interests as important and is shown to boost group-serving behaviour when it's present in the brain" [78]. Oxytocin also soothes our survival system by interrupting the amygdala, lowering cortisol levels, anxiety and blood pressure [79]. So, instead of preparing to respond to the threat of others, our nervous system registers the intrinsically rewarding nature of being connected with them.

Building on this, let's look at some other advice for enabling inclusion in your boardroom.

Advice on harnessing diversity

Awareness: Acknowledging your defensive and inclusive brain states

In this chapter, we've seen how the beliefs and assumptions that shape our view of a situation are encoded in the neural connections in our brain, influencing the way we absorb and interpret information, and biasing our decisions. In Part One we also examined the psychological defence mechanisms we use under pressure. For example, simplifying a situation into the polarised options of split thinking, where things are either good or bad, right or wrong, friend or foe. We've now suggested such defences may have some of their neurological roots in survival circuits, which ready us to deal with perceived threat. And we've observed that our nervous system's survival tactics have physical components and noticeable effects on our brain's ability to function.

For these reasons, Casey and Robinson advocate developing the habit of tuning into the state of your brain. They suggest actively noticing when the state of your mind is defensive, which can manifest itself as "a tendency to deflect and blame others or external circumstances for problems or issues" [75]. They also encourage developing your awareness of what effect this has on your mental functioning. For instance, people commonly report struggling to see options, make conscious choices, and take constructive action when they are feeling defensive – which is consistent with the impact of stress chemicals on the brain (as discussed earlier). Crucially, it's also usually difficult to listen to others. The tricky aspect is that these effects decrease your ability to notice what's happening to you and manage the impact. In other words, when you most need this capacity, it's least available to you.

So it's wise to be vigilant to the ways in which your ability to behave inclusively toward others is being hampered by your own in-built biases and defensive reactions. It's sensible to pay attention to your capacity for curiosity, compassion, creativity and respectful engagement across differences. Strengthening these faculties, and the neurochemical and neural pathways that support them, can enable you to harness diversity on your board. Our interviewees gave examples of what this can look like in practice.

One cross-cultural board advisor explained that the usual approach of trying to learn about the cultures of other board members has its limitations. *"If you're a US board member and there's a Chinese chairman, you read about the Chinese, right?"* But the thing it's important to understand is your *own* culture, how your biases and preferences may appear to people from other cultures, and how your behaviour might be hard to understand or trigger their threat responses. He added, *"the problem is you"* because *"the hardest culture to understand has to be your own because 'I don't have a culture. I just have common sense.'"* In other words, you see your own world view as the norm, and tend to assume others share it, when in fact they may see things very differently. He advocates becoming aware of your own cultural bias. Being alert to how you differ culturally from others over things like comfort with public challenge, expectations of airtime in relation to hierarchy, the amount of social time and speed of decision-making.

The next step is making your underlying assumptions explicit to others and available for discussion to aid mutual understanding. Like the characters in our inside story, who leapt ahead assuming shared understanding, we often need to ensure we are really on the same page as people who are different from us. A non-executive describes this happening across different professions on boards. Watching HR professionals, CFOs and General Counsel talking, he said

> *they all come with incredibly insightful wisdom but it's almost myopic. And then what usually happens is they presume everybody knows what they know.*

Our interviewee knew that these specialists' views were built on decades of experience. For example, *"30 years of being a General Counsel"* or *"47 trade union negotiations."* He advises those with this level of expertise to consider their colleagues' experience, then take their time to lay out their underlying reasoning. This enables the rest of the board to really *"appreciate the value [these professionals] are adding in their role diversity."*

You may have to work hard to make yourself aware of your inherent assumptions at first, because the underpinnings of your own thought processes can seem so obvious that you can't see them, or don't view them as worth expressing. As we've already seen, the neural set-up in your own brain is your only way to engage with the world, and it's hard to imagine different mindsets hewn from others' genes and varied experiences. But sharing your thought processes and assumptions with others is useful in itself and encourages colleagues to do the same in return. This opens up an exploration of differences that can be remarkably fertile ground for developing concepts or solutions informed by multiple perspectives.

Crucial questions – Awareness

- Is my brain in a defensive or inclusive state right now?
- What's obvious to me that others might not see?

Relating: Developing inclusive habits

Bringing multiple perspectives to interactions

One of our interviewees – an academic with board experience – noted that colleagues who are good at the habit we've just described (holding the beliefs and perspectives of others in mind) often promote boardroom inclusion by, in effect, acting as translators. They notice points of mutual incomprehension between colleagues by seeing the discussion from both sides, spotting the gaps, and making them explicit and discussable. This academic notes that deliberately engineering opportunities for people to see the world from a variety of perspectives – early in their careers – helps them develop this habit, giving them experiences that will enrich their neural pathways. For example, rotating people through functions and geographies in multi-national organisations is a powerful way of developing this skill in future board members. By the time you're in your mid-career *"you know how to talk to finance people and marketing people, you've worked in China, worked in South America"* and you can hold these perspectives in mind as you interact. Similarly, board members who have varied and unconventional life or career histories – those who have emigrated from their birth country, studied unusual subject combinations, or moved between functions or types of organisations – are likely to be open to fresh perspectives.

Discussing differences

However mindful you are of difference, there will be times when it's hard to appreciate other points of view, and easy to stumble into a sensitive area and cause offence. When this happens, it's crucial to take action to protect and strengthen relationships. A *Harvard Business Review* article on diversity and board performance improvement explains the importance of acknowledging "mishaps in communication" [80]. Discussing issues frankly as they emerge, rather than shying away from them, is immensely important, but can feel fraught with danger. In line with neuroscientific theory, one public sector executive puts this down to threat and fear.

> *When I have raised issues of race or gender, the awkwardness levels in the room have hit the roof ... I think people are worried about being labelled racist or sexist or homophobic or whatever.*

She advocates *"getting those issues out on the table quite early on in your relationship with somebody"* and recommends talking about how you are different and how that might show up in the way you relate to others on your board. This executive offers some advice about these uncomfortable conversations. *"I don't think you can learn it through training, but you can learn it through wanting to get to know somebody."*

Crucial questions – Relating

- What experiences could help current and potential board members expand their world view?
- How are you and I different and what does that mean for how we interact and work together?

We describe next a power tool that can help you channel your natural curiosity and desire for connection in defensive moments.

Power tool: SAVE Communication Model™

The SAVE Communication Model™ was developed by Casey and Murphy Robinson as a four-step process to help your curious, clear, thinking self to stay active and maintain positive regard for others [75]. You can use it to 'save' a conversation in which perceived threats have triggered your defences, leading to negative feelings and narrow thinking. Instead, the model helps to produce the brain chemicals that aid trust and bonding between individuals, restoring the brain conditions for working creatively and constructively together. In uncomfortable situations they recommend that you:

Stop what you're doing and focus on the other person.

Placing your full attention on someone has a powerful effect on them and you. In a busy world, it's unusual – and rewarding – to be fully seen and heard by someone. It's particularly powerful for people who have experienced marginalisation or discrimination. When you stop and pay attention to someone, you send an unequivocal message of value and respect, triggering positive brain chemicals like oxytocin, as we described above.

Ask questions that encourage others to speak.

Posing open questions from a place of genuine curiosity also stimulates positive emotions, associated with reward, in the nervous systems of both questioner and questioned. Couching your questions in non-threatening ways, with warm and open tone and body language, enables open dialogue and mutual understanding. We explore how to do this further in the *Tactics* section below.

Validate and don't interrupt.

Listening in order to validate involves a conscious intention to hear what the other person has to say, sense what they mean and tune into how they feel. It involves putting your own reactions and potential responses temporarily to one side. It means avoiding the temptation to interrupt and instead letting pauses, and even silences, linger. It's about opening up space for someone to express themselves fully on their own terms, so that they feel heard.

End with explicit positive regard.

Finishing a conversation with a sincere expression of appreciation for the person, and the interaction you've just had, communicates your ongoing regard and commitment to your relationship. Particularly when a conversation has been difficult, acknowledging this and expressing appreciation for what's emerged, and their willingness to talk, makes both parties more likely to stay engaged in the future.

What other techniques can help you operate more inclusively? Here are some suggestions from our research.

Tactics: Creating the conditions for inclusive dialogue

Diversifying recruitment processes

The first condition for harnessing diversity is having a good range of perspectives around the board table in the first place, and your approach to recruitment has a key role to play in this. As we mentioned in the *Are you noticing?* section, our research revealed that it's not unusual for board opportunities to be "*passed through social networks, and people encourage their own protégé or their own mentee whom they have a connection with.*" This restricts the range of people who hear about roles, and can also place people with connections in poll position. For example, when a sponsor grooms someone by "*meeting socially several times as a prelude to the official interview, which is then just a bit of a formality.*" Our interviewee panel advises that more transparency, creativity and specialist support in your recruitment process can help.

Setting out a structured process for application and selection helps potential candidates see a way in, and gives people further down in the organisation a visible pathway. Clear selection criteria, and a robust process for evaluating candidates, also mitigates your neurally based affinity with people who are similar to you. Commissioning search and selection experts, such as head-hunters, can bring additional rigour to the process, and there is a growing range of professionals who specialise in helping organisations recruit candidates with specific characteristics. As one advises *"The more structure you can have, the more transparency you can have, and the more you can hold everyone to account for maintaining that."*

So how can you encourage people who bring real new perspectives to apply for positions on your board? This is where some context-sensitive creativity is needed to attract a range of talent. Several boards report combing their markets and customer groups for potential colleagues and finding this pays dividends in the representation of characteristics like age, ethnicity and socio-economic group. One international academic institution looked to the alumni of its programmes for individuals with board potential, and a public sector body chose to include employee representatives. Several charity non-executives backed the idea of board members who had lived experience of the issues that the charity was tackling, to inject this vital viewpoint. Others had experimented with shadow boards, or sub-groups, to involve people close to the issues, while giving them useful committee and board-like experience. These board members shared the sentiment that these kinds of initiatives have the potential to *"really make us reflect on what we're trying to do as an organisation ... and we'll keep pushing them and it will drive change."*

Matching your markets

If your organisation has global reach or aspirations, our interviewees advise ensuring that you have board members who understand the different territories. They see real value in the ability of multi-lingual and multi-national members to understand how staff, customers, stakeholders and competitors tend to think, feel and respond in a particular geography or culture. One UK-based chair offered a blunt warning: *"If you've got an English board and you've got a multi-national business then you're nuts."* In addition to insights about local conditions, a board advisor notes strong evidence to suggest that people from different countries bring varied ways of framing and thinking about problems. As the cross-cultural researcher Geert Hofstede identified, there are a number of dimensions to this. These include different beliefs, including assumptions about how power is distributed within hierarchies, and the benefits of collectivism compared with individualism. They also include different preferences, for example, for traditionally masculine versus feminine traits, for how much uncertainty is tolerated, and for long-term rather than short-term orientation [81]. Such variety is likely to add breadth and depth to boardroom discussion.

Signalling permission and encouragement

Once you have assembled a diverse board, there was general agreement that the chair has a key role in creating an inclusive environment in the boardroom and beyond. A culture of psychological safety, where people feel free to be themselves and share their views without fear of reprisals, is a good general aim. We suggested a power tool for generating this sense of security in Chapter 1. An important aspect of this is inviting board colleagues' participation, and several interviewees reflected on how best to go about this, and the impact of your approach and tone. For example "*Asking 'what's the female perspective on this?' might feel quite inclusive to the chair, by inviting in the other*" but it can have "*the opposite effect.*"

Some of our interviewees reported that even within groups which are committed to diversity, equality and inclusion, this type of framing primes the room "*to think, 'Oh, this is a person who speaks about minority issues.'*" Much like the token gestures we described in the *Are you noticing?* section, it stimulates the neurons related to a stereotype in the minds of listeners. Board members' quick, automatic evaluations of what their female colleague says may then be negatively biased by discriminatory associations. It might also trigger a *stereotype threat* in the woman herself, which is when a person's survival circuits are triggered by fears about conforming to a prejudiced view about a group to which they belong. Both neurological effects "*potentially marginalise the rest of what she might talk about.*"

The advice to chairs is to take a stance with the board members, namely "*you should be allowed to speak because everyone should be allowed to speak.*" And be "*aware that there are many unconscious biases in the room that might be at play, and it's on [the chair] to do something about that*" in the way they manage discussions. One chair noted that to do this effectively "*you've got to actively want the contribution and be patient*" since colleagues' contributions may come out as "*cross and angry and frustrated*" because of strongly held views and feelings. They are also sometimes accompanied by overtones of the seesaw, standoff, and bullying dynamics we explored in Part One. This means that the more varied your board, the more you may have to engage your self-awareness and relating skills to get the best from each member.

Doing this often involves another component of psychological safety: ensuring that you respond constructively to colleagues. One chair describes a scene from her diverse board, comprising people who bring the employee perspective as well as those of senior executives and non-executives. "*Recently at a debate about diversity and the positive action we are prepared to take, one of my board members* said, "*I feel as though I was told I was wrong just because I didn't hold the same view as you.*" The chair saw it as her job to praise her colleague "*for actually voicing that and being up front because it's quite tough to say amongst a lot of colleagues.*" Other members of the board were supportive too, saying "*No, it's not that you're wrong, this is a tricky subject. There are going to be a diverse range of views.*" Other chairs reported saying that there are no "*daft questions*" or "*odd ideas*" at their board, and even contributing a few themselves to lead the way. They use this invitation to demonstrate that board members are welcome to bring things from outside the mainstream. These permission signals send a strongly inclusive message.

In addition to reinforcement in the moment, board members reported giving or receiving encouragement outside the boardroom. One described an informal conversation with their CEO "*who clearly demonstrated to me their deeply held beliefs and values about gender and race*" and views that anyone could achieve anything. This inspired her confidence in him – and in herself. Another non-executive notes that they consciously choose "*not to get irritated with people who say very little, and outside meetings try to find out the reasons why.*" The non-executive reported having a very practical conversation, along the lines of "*how would you like to contribute?*" Building these kinds of questions into board evaluation processes can be useful, as can asking people about any obstacles to participation that they observe.

Balancing advocacy with enquiry

We've seen already that our research identified dialogue as an important tool for overcoming barriers and working through differences. One board advisor explains that

> *Boards can either be arenas where you go into it trying to make shared sense of a problem, or you go into it trying to win an argument.*

In the dialogue approach, participants are aware that they hold different positions, with varied underlying frames of reference, and they respect this difference. Often this involves quelling their threat response and consciously choosing a more curious and appreciative attitude. As we described earlier, individuals can then be open about their assumptions and hold up their ideas for inspection and exploration by others, who actively enquire into them. Through this inclusive exchange, they extend each other's perceptions and thinking.

Most board dialogue involves a combination of advocacy and enquiry. It can be illuminating to pay specific attention to the balance between the two, to foster a healthy discussion that draws on broad perspectives. How much airtime is spent advocating ideas or positions on a topic, and how much do board colleagues ask questions of others, to really understand their concept or point of view? Where there are questions, are these veiled ways of reinforcing a position, or genuine attempts to understand why people around the table think and feel differently? Fundamentally, it's important to discover if members are tapping into each other's experiences and expertise to extend their shared understanding of a subject, or just pushing their own position to win the argument.

It's worth noting that enquiry can be just as daunting as advocacy. But the positive interest it conveys is likely to trigger your reward and attachment brain chemicals, rather than triggering your survival circuits through competition. This means that everyone around the table is more likely to feel orientated towards collaboration – with all the physiological benefits that brings – than to feel constrained by reactions to threat. Our panel had various ideas for rebalancing your board towards enquiry. Several chairs designated some agenda items as exploratory, to explicitly signal the appropriateness of open-minded enquiry into the subject. Other board members actively modelled enquiry themselves, asking high-quality enquiry questions, particularly of colleagues whom others were struggling to understand. Questions like *"Can you tell me more about your thinking behind that idea?"*, *"How do you feel about my concerns?"* and *"Where do you see our main points of difference?"* And one experienced chair noted that whilst an enquiry mode can be more time-consuming than advocacy, making time on your agenda for full discussions is vital to harness the full range of perspectives.

Crucial questions – Tactics

- Do we have the optimum balance of advocacy and enquiry in our discussion of this topic?
- How can we ensure inclusive dialogue?

Investing for the long term

We noted in the introduction to this chapter that, despite apparent willingness to improve diversity on boards, progress has been sluggish. This may be because some corrective actions take many years to show results, making them less of a priority for boards looking for short-term returns. Nonetheless, our panel advise you to think ahead. In one non-executive's words *"If you want to bring diversity into the boardroom, you don't want to be worrying about which women or which ethnic groups you hire tomorrow."* To increase the supply of talent to your board in the future, you need to look at the pipeline of *"people who are 35 and going 'how do I get this person who's functionally excellent and create an environment in which they flourish [and] really use their capability.'"* Challenge yourself and your organisation to find this diverse talent early and support their development.

Solutions include programmes that address attrition at specific career points for some demographic groups, or spot and nurture early career board potential in people who have characteristics that are under-represented at the most senior levels. Or you can begin even earlier, working with social enterprises that specialise in implementing mentoring, internships, or C-suite shadowing schemes for people who may face barriers to boardroom entry. Activities like this are unlikely to significantly shift the diversity dial immediately, but they can serve as a beacon of inclusivity, attracting diverse employees to all levels of your organisation.

Summary

Harnessing diversity is hard

It's important that boards recruit members with varied characteristics and operate inclusively to use their perspectives and insights. Despite growing consensus on the advantages of diverse boards, progress towards them is slow. This is because positive action has long-term pay-offs, and despite conscious good intentions, your nervous system harbours in-built bias.

Homogenous boards

Some boards are like echo chambers in which members reinforce each other's restricted views. Efforts to improve this can be tick-box exercises, and even if a range of characteristics is represented, members can be or feel excluded or marginalised.

The physiology of bias

Your nervous system is shaped by your genes and experiences, which determine the wiring of your neural pathways. These affect the way you interpret information and take decisions and can build in bias against people who are different from you. Your brain perceives difference as threatening. Your survival circuits, centred on your amygdala, respond with brain chemicals like cortisol, prompting defensiveness. You can consciously choose to override your biases and adopt an inclusive attitude that encourages hormones like oxytocin, which promote attachment. With practice, new ways of interacting become habitual – hard wired into your brain.

Awareness: Acknowledge your defensive brain state

Your brain and body chemistry is dynamic and determines your thoughts, emotions and actions. You can notice your state of mind and manage it, so that you become less preoccupied by threat and stress. To achieve this, spend more time accessing brain functions like focused attention, appreciation of other perspectives and making conscious choices. These capabilities enable collaboration with people from whom you are different, as well as improving access to your cognitive skills.

Relating: Develop inclusive habits

Your ability to bear in mind the perspective of others is a key skill. It enables you to adapt sufficiently to bridge gaps and tap into fresh worldviews. Working in diverse teams can be challenging and sometimes you will misunderstand or offend each other. It's important to talk about your differences, even if it's uncomfortable, and actively look for ways to accommodate each other.

Tactics: Create conditions for open dialogue

Structured and transparent recruitment processes, and creative thinking about how to attract candidates, can help you recruit board members with diverse characteristics. Investing in initiatives for the long term will improve diversity for future generations. In board meetings, actively signal permission for people to contribute, and aim for dialogue rather than debate.

Power tool: SAVE Communication Model™

You can 'save' a conversation where you are reacting defensively by focusing on the other person, asking questions which encourage them to speak, then listening to and validating their perspective. Ending interactions with appreciation and positive regard strengthens bonds for future interactions.

Further reading

Diversity, Inclusion and Belonging in Coaching: A Practical Guide Book by Salma Shah.
Rebel Ideas: The Power of Diverse Thinking by Matthew Syed.
The Neuroscience of Inclusion: New Skills for New Times by Mary Casey and Shannon Murphy Robinson.

Chapter 7

Facing up to a doomsday scenario

It's a completely different mindset running a business that's going down. If you're in free fall ... it's like being a peace time Prime Minister and the next minute you're right in the trenches. It really is a fundamental change.

Chair, hospitality group

Introduction

In a previous chapter we looked at insular, ivory tower boards that have lost touch with their organisation and markets, and often fail to foresee obvious problems. This can have serious consequences, including doomsday scenarios, in which the very existence of the enterprise is called into question. Crisis situations can also be caused by external events that aren't easily anticipated, such as the Covid-19 pandemic, geo-political conflict, climate-related events or changes in government policy. Often a combination of internal and external factors come together to create a 'perfect storm' and a real risk that an organisation will fail. So it's not surprising that most of our interviewees had encountered some sort of doomsday scenario. These ranged from financial difficulties, looming criminal prosecutions and radical restructures to regulator-enforced special measures.

Board members discovered that things go wrong surprisingly quickly, requiring some *"pretty decisive management"* from the board. As our interviewee the board advisor and author Margaret Heffernan noted *"Companies are like humans they can be hail and healthy one minute or ailing the next if the board is not paying attention."* You only have to look at the sudden fall from grace of previously high-profile companies like Enron or Lehman Brothers, or more recently Carillion in the UK and Wirecard in Germany, to confirm this. Data from the UK Office for National Statistics and the US Bureau of Labor Statistics 2019 and 2021 respectively shows that a fifth of new businesses fail in their first two years, rising to 65% in the first 10 years. When our interviewees found this happening to their organisation they described it as *"deeply shocking"* and a *"horrible experience,"* which they *"never*

DOI: 10.4324/9780429340239-11

thought would happen" to them. Individual board members can feel personal fear and become focused on self-preservation. Fuelled by the belief, as one director put it, that *"you're only as good as your reputation. And once your reputation has gone, you have nothing."*

Managing such unstable and chaotic situations can become fully time consuming for an intense period. A non-executive who was part of an institution's rescue team during the global financial crisis described a typical scenario. Their involvement went from 30 days plus 8 annual board meetings a year, to meetings every day for 12 months. And if you've always run an organisation that has functioned well, it can be hard to adjust in other ways. A crisis may require a completely different mindset and skills, as we'll discuss in this chapter. The pressure of catastrophic situations can result in colleagues exhibiting unexpected behaviours, which vary between individuals. You might see a totally different side to members whom you thought you knew well. A non-executive in a government regulator likens it to soldiers who *"until they go into battle, you have no idea how they're really going to react to live fire."* As a director in one doomsday scenario witnessed,

> *some colleagues were ostrich-like, but I also saw incredible selflessness. Some really wanted the organisation to survive and would do a lot to make this happen and others were last in the line.*

It brings out the best and worst in people.

And this happens at a time when the board's reaction to the threatening situation can be pivotal to the organisation's survival. Because *"if you have a board that's quasi-dysfunctional, you exacerbate the situation for management."* Whereas *"a cohesive, thoughtful board"* can help bring clarity and calm. In boards that were perceived as working well in knife-edge circumstances *"everybody was trying to help, there was no shirking, nobody ducking, nobody trying to get out early."* You're all pulling together, with a good team of competent advisers, and you have trust in each other. All members of the board are playing their part, in different ways, to solve the problems.

In this chapter we cover what neuroscience can tell us about these contrasting reactions, which seem poles apart. We look at how actual and perceived threats in doomsday scenarios trigger the brain and nervous system, impacting people in different, and sometimes surprising ways. And we consider what your board can do to work together well in a crisis.

Let's see first, in more detail, the range of behaviour you might notice from board members.

What are you noticing? Responses to a doomsday scenario

Denying or distancing from the problem

Some boards find it hard to accept the gravity of their situation. The board of a construction company were *"congratulating themselves on their strategic genius"* for taking the decision to diversify into sustainable green energy systems, such as heat pumps and solar panels. As the months went on, the costs of investment in this new area escalated, and the cash forecasts showed money haemorrhaging from the business. The board chair and executive continued to deny how bad the situation was, refusing to accept that their strategic decision had imperilled the company. They were eventually forced to accept a takeover bid from a competitor, who quickly shut down this unprofitable part of the enterprise.

Board members described other situations in which colleagues could see the problem, but did not face up to it. Some continued *"clinging on to an untenable narrative about the past"* as things spiralled more and more out of control. Others described fellow board members becoming *"a bit paralysed ... and just kind of overwhelmed by the situation."* It was almost as if they were *"shutting down"* and unable to act and make decisions. One board coach observed that, in their long career, another telltale sign of this was when members of the board felt dependent on external advisers. Taking the attitude, for example, that *"we'll get PwC in to solve the issue and all will be well."*

In one case, because of a change in government policy, there was a complete restructuring of a government service over 18 months. Part of the service was closed down and hived off to the private sector, leading to high rates of staff attrition, redundancies and low morale. The CEO of the board tasked with delivering this policy to dismantle their organisation, described the board as doing so in a *"robotic"* way. They explained that *"as a board and as a senior leadership team, we just did that unquestioningly"* as a coping mechanism. Faced with breaking up a well-performing organisation for political reasons, they shut off their emotions because *"we all thought that if you allowed conflict to surface, it wouldn't be helpful for the organisation to be able to carry on doing its good work"* in the meantime.

An alternative way of avoiding terminal difficulties is to leave the organisation. Board members saw colleagues *"plotting their exits"* as soon as things got tough, and there was a risk that the organisation would not survive. To fellow board members this behaviour seemed driven by the fear of reputational damage. Non-executive directors were observed complaining that this wasn't what they *"signed up for. So I'm resigning."* Others commented that they were not being paid enough or were not prepared to devote the necessary time to the emerging issues.

Playing the blame game

Another common response is those under pressure pinning blame for the crisis here, there and everywhere. Perhaps on colleagues (particularly the senior management team), or on external factors, such as an economic downturn or an increase in the cost of commodities. Interviewees described this like a *"flinging match"* with cumulative allegations that *"this is wrong and this, and then what about this?"* It could go as far as the non-executives having an *"I told you so"* attitude towards the executive. A coach observed seeing colleagues on boards in trouble *"just finding other people to kick"* to make themselves feel better. Venting their emotions and shouting at others as a relief from their own misery. In a case where a multinational faced criminal charges for allegedly breaching government trading sanctions, some of the non-executive directors were incredulous as to how the executives had got the company into this situation. They blamed their executive colleagues for exposing the organisation and its individual office holders to criminal proceedings.

Reassuringly frank interviewees also admitted tussles with their own consciences, self-flagellating over their role in causing the problem and wondering if they were partly to blame. Why had they missed things and what, with hindsight, could they have done better? Crisis management involves difficult judgement calls, and board members mentioned deliberating over whether they should have done something differently. For example, the incoming chair of a charity, who had been a trustee of the organisation for a few months previously, was thrown into a Charity Commission investigation of poor governance by the previous management team. He chastised himself because, with hindsight *"there were enough signs that we were in dangerous territory,"* but on becoming chair *"I just discovered it was more dangerous than I realised. By the time I discovered that it was too late."*

Behaving unethically

The stress of dangerous circumstances can also lead to extremely unscrupulous behaviour – what one interviewee described as fellow board members showing their *"true colours."* This was more than the angry or domineering reactions that we encountered earlier in the standoff or bullying chapters. For example, one director of a start-up company, which for months had fought to stay afloat, was horrified by his colleagues' actions when the receivers were brought in. They had worked together as equity partners in the company, but suddenly developed a dog-eat-dog attitude. They were acting *"inappropriately, to put it mildly, and started to do things that were potentially illegal."* When it became clear that the business was going under, the directors were taking the opportunity to strip the assets and to use them to start up a new enterprise. They collected office equipment, harvested data for their own use, changed locks and passwords, and generally acted in unscrupulous ways. His shock was surpassed only when years later one of them asked for a reference for a new role, apparently unaware of, or unabashed by, their questionable actions.

Leaning in

There are some board members who channel their energy into stepping up to the plate and leading the disaster response, rather than avoiding it, blaming others or behaving problematically. A trustee who was an accountant by training, and chair of an audit committee, recounts having to be more operational when financial crisis loomed at a charity. The trustee realised early on that the new CFO, who appeared nervous at meetings, was out of his depth and "*not really up to the job.*" That trustee subsequently unearthed that the CFO was misrepresenting the cash-flow figures. On discovering the figures were wrong, the trustee took charge of the detailed negotiations with the bank to obtain further funding and led the recruitment of a replacement CFO. He saw this as his duty until the crisis had passed, and he could return to his usual trustee responsibilities.

Another director realised that her company was facing the kind of 'perfect storm' we described in the introduction to this chapter. A combination of several factors spelt trouble, including a serious funding gap caused by changes to their markets, a lack of a coherent strategy and succession issues. She seemed to be the only one on the board who saw it coming and "*jumped on it.*" She had detailed meetings with the management team to come up with possible solutions. Having taken these soundings, she then saw her role as a "*critical friend, talking to the chair and steering him to address these issues.*"

Health effect

We've seen in previous chapters that stressful situations can have physiological effects. In some cases, the sudden shock of receiving crisis news can have an immediate physical impact. This short-term pressure reaction is commonly called *acute stress*. For example, a chair of school governors collapsed at a meeting, surprised by the news that school inspectors were putting the school into special measures because of its failings. He was taken to hospital, complaining of chest pains.

In other doomsday scenarios, the trauma of disastrous events unfolding over a long period can lead some people to suffer from long-term health conditions. In these drawn-out situations, individuals can suffer what is known as long-term *chronic stress*, with ongoing day-to-day physical results. As coaches we've worked with executive team members who are under such continuous crisis pressure and experience sleepless nights, migraines, eczema or panic attacks. Our coach panel had also worked with board members where prolonged exposure to a doomsday

Table 7.1 What are you noticing? The doomsday scenario

Avoiding the issue	Refusing to acknowledge the impending crisis, stepping back and withdrawing from the situation, or looking to external advisors for help.
Pointing the finger	Board members blaming colleagues, external factors or in some cases themselves for the crisis.
Unscrupulous actions	Board members unexpectedly behaving illegally and selfishly for their own preservation.
Your health suffering	Feeling unwell and having physical symptoms during and following intense pressure at work.
Taking over	Individuals on the board determined to fix matters and dominating the action.

scenario had led to even more severe physical and mental health problems. These include individuals who have taken leave because of long-term illness and are working on their well-being to return to full health and work. The serious impact of long-term pressure is not surprising, as research shows that it increases susceptibility to heart disease and cancer [63].

You can see from these wide responses that each person's reaction to fear and pressure varies greatly. Table 7.1 is a quick reference review of the common responses you may find when board members face a doomsday scenario.

Inside story: Stormy seas

The chair of a family-run swimwear business had been at the helm for five decades. This creative, entrepreneurial founder was a larger-than-life character and had built a well-known high-end label. With the founder as executive chair and CEO, the brand had made significant investments in developing other product lines, such as skin care and beach-style homeware products. As one of his colleagues on the board wryly observed, the chair was always drawn to "*shiny new things*" but struggled to see them through. As a result, 80% of the business focused on design, production and distribution to their original European swimwear market.

The current board of this private company included several generations of the founder's family, including two of the chair's grand-daughters. There were also two non-family directors, including the CFO. But given that most of the directors were related to the chair and of a much younger generation, it didn't really feel like a board of equals. A cash-flow pattern emerged over the years, with much of the revenue generated in the European summer months. With the help of one of the younger grand-daughter directors, the business had started to overhaul its outdated financial and supply chain management systems, financing the investment through a substantial loan. At this point, the founder, a lifelong music lover, announced that he had struck an expensive deal for the brand to sponsor a series of summer music festivals at European coastal resorts. The CFO eyed this second investment with scepticism, as the last decade had seen a gradual weakening in the cash position of the organisation, and he did not believe it would see a good return.

Within a few weeks, the Covid-19 global pandemic struck, leading governments to impose restrictions on travel and socialising. Demand fell as customers were no longer taking holidays, and the music festivals were postponed. As debts mounted, unpaid creditors were threatening to wind up the company. Its representatives in Asia, where many of its products were manufactured, were being physically intimidated because of unpaid debts, and one even received a death threat. Some of the older family members started staying away from tense crisis board meetings, where often tempers frayed. They didn't seem to take the situation seriously until the "*bomb went off as it were*" and then were nowhere to be seen. They cited various reasons for staying away. One said that the arguments were "*affecting their nerves*" and they were too mentally exhausted to attend; another that they didn't think their input was needed as they trusted the founder implicitly and he would sort it out, as he'd done before. One of the younger grand-daughter directors announced she was leaving the board to take a long-planned sabbatical.

The founder remained relentlessly optimistic about the brand he'd built over his lifetime. He thought that any problems were just a phase, and the business would turn the corner. However, the younger generation of the family could see that the business was teetering on the brink and that the "*doomsday scenario was beginning to appear over the horizon.*" The CFO observed that "*you could see the family were really trying to find a way out for [the founder] that was not humiliating, frankly.*" The founder became hard to contact, ignoring calls or emails between board meetings. His only contribution to the debate was a string of suggestions for new product categories to bridge the gap. But these ideas were blocked by the grand-daughter and CFO who could see that the company lacked sufficient cash to invest in them. Instead, they wanted to cut costs and appoint new accountants to advise on restructuring the business. Things came to a head at a crunch board meeting, with the founder and his grand-daughter at loggerheads, while other members observed, passive and uneasy. The founder, hurt, angry and blaming the rest of the board for a lack of faith and vision, tendered his resignation and stormed out.

What happened next

Throughout this time, supply chain creditors were threatening to push the company into liquidation and press any liquidator to take the founder and other office holders to court for trading whilst knowingly insolvent. The younger generation of board members were determined to face their problems and fight for the family business.

They formed a steering group with the CFO and a newly appointed interim chair, to devise and execute a survival strategy. This group met daily for months, reporting back to the main board regularly. Their new financial advisors pointed out the unrealised potential of some of their undeveloped product lines, particularly homeware. They also suggested different business models like licensing, to generate cash swiftly. The steering group committed to work together on restructuring their core business, whilst forming new commercial partnerships to unlock liquidity. They commissioned several rapid pilots to market-test a range of options, keeping a close eye on emerging results to inform decisions about whether to scale, adapt or stop each one.

It was touch and go, but the business did weather the storm, pay creditors and emerge from the crisis commercially stronger. The combination of properly diversified product lines, and a new business model which leveraged the brand, made for a more profitable enterprise. Despite this, the fallout within the family created rifts which didn't heal – certain family members never sat around the same boardroom or dining room table again.

What are the neuroscientific reasons for board members behaving so differently in the face of extreme pressure? We look now at the impact of stress on your nervous system.

Psychological roots: Our survival mode in stressful situations

Our automatic and learnt responses to threat

In the previous chapter we saw that our nervous system responds to perceived threats in our environment in ways intended to ensure our survival. A crisis in an organisation is another example of a threat which can cause the release of brain chemicals, to help manage the perceived pressure. These chemicals can activate several other aspects of the body's threat responses. For example, the acute stress of an out-of-the-blue shock can trigger an automatic *fight or flight* response [74]. Walter Canon first used this term to describe an immediate, unthinking, active response to a perceived threat, where we instinctively attack back or run away from a situation. Another reflex response when threatened is to *freeze* (like an animal hoping that it's not going to be detected). As the neuroscientist Joseph LeDoux explains in his broad-ranging book *Anxious: The Modern Mind in the Age of Anxiety*, this immobility serves the purpose of using as little energy as possible [74]. And in extreme circumstances, where we perceive there is no other option, our body may shut down completely, becoming unresponsive and even paralysed. This is known as *tonic immobility*, or colloquially as flopping (like the board member we described collapsing in the previous *Are you noticing?* section). In a sudden crisis, these alternative fight, flight, freeze and flop reactions can vary from colleague to colleague.

Board members exposed to the difficulties of doomsday scenarios which unfold over many months may also encounter chronic stress – the effects of continual pressure over the long term. Here, to cope when we feel threatened by uncertainty and lack of control, we lean on learnt habits to avoid distress and make ourselves feel better. These habits are encoded in our brain through associations between experiences of pressure and actions we have taken to relieve unpleasant feelings in the past. A simple example is the habit of having a glass of wine at the end of a difficult day. It's an instance of the Hebbian learning that we described in Chapter 6. When we've taken a course of action that has served us well previously, and our brain predicts that a threat is a similar situation, we're predisposed to take that approach again. It's a self-reinforcing process, as the more we repeat the pattern, the more our brain's wiring of that neural pathway is strengthened. This primes us to keep responding to particular stressors in our environment by behaving in a certain way.

So present-day reactions are shaped by past experiences of responding to pressure. As the neuroscientist Lisa Feldman Barrett succinctly explains, experiences you make today become your brain predictions for tomorrow [63]. This gives each of us our own personal playbook of survival behaviour and explains the range of responses we outlined in the *Are you noticing?* section above. We might take a course of action – distancing ourselves from the board, fighting our corner or stepping-in and taking charge – because it's helped us cope with pressure before. Or our go to method of surviving a threat might be to keep our head down and avoid being noticed, as that's kept us safe in the past.

Next, we explore what's happening in our nervous system in acute and chronic stress situations, and the short- and long-term impacts this can have on actions, well-being and health.

Our bodies' responses to threats

The neurons, in the part of our bodies' nervous systems called the *autonomic nervous system*, help manage our responses to threats. This system consists of neurons outside and parallel to the spinal cord that control and regulate the heart, lungs, blood vessels and digestion. The autonomic nervous system has two branches, the first being the *sympathetic nervous system*, named after the Greek word for feeling or emotion. This is stimulated when our amygdala detects a threat using information from our senses and prompts us to react. This is the physiological basis of the fight or flight response we've described previously. Heart rate and blood pressure increase because, amongst other things, brain chemicals like adrenaline and cortisol are released, increasing arousal and energy. And cortisol also helps working memory in the short term, so we are more productive in dealing with an immediate threat in acute stress situations.

In contrast, the second branch of the autonomic nervous system, the *parasympathetic nervous system* (meaning "against emotions") works to slow down metabolism and pace the body's nervous mechanisms. This branch is commonly known as the rest and digest system. It reduces heart rate, relaxes muscles and slows breathing and blood flows to the digestive organs. The parasympathetic mode is active when we are relaxed, in safe and non-threatening situations, but can also play a role in our threat response. When the parasympathetic system becomes more dominant than the action-orientated, sympathetic mode, we are more likely to have a freeze response to acute threats – being immobile, shutting down and dissociating from the threat to protect ourselves and conserve energy.

Because of their different roles, the sympathetic and parasympathetic autonomic nervous system branches are sometimes referred to as the body's accelerator and brake respectively [82]. They help us survive and regulate the body's energy, but if the two branches are out of kilter, particularly over a long time, this can have physical and mental repercussions. The autonomic nervous system response evolved to deal with transitory threats, and when we experience stress over an extended period, it causes continual high levels of stress chemicals, such as cortisol. This has the damaging physical effect of weakening the immune system, making us prone to frequent illness. Prolonged exposure to the neurochemicals associated with stress can also lead to insomnia, reduce working memory and limit our ability to think clearly and solve problems. This happens, for instance, when our sympathetic nervous system is stuck in accelerator survival mode – when the body can't determine the significance of threats, perceives them all to be significant, and is continually ready for defensive action. In the longer term, this can result in someone being in a constant state of panic, and at risk of burn out and depression [83].

Balancing your autonomic nervous system

How our bodies learn to respond to pressure depends on our personality, our memories and the consequences of past threats. But as we've seen already, the good news is that our nervous system, including the brain, is adaptable. We can change it, for example using the self-efficacy strategies we discussed in the rubber stamp chapter. Research shows that people who are most resilient in difficult situations will have a suite of approaches that help them cope, and are flexible in choosing the most appropriate in the circumstances [74]. Here neuroscience reveals the benefits of top-down and bottom-up approaches. The former involve consciously engaging our cognitive capacities by increasing focus and self-awareness, while the latter help physically to bring the body's autonomic nervous system into a healthy balance. Bessel van der Kolk comprehensively reviews these approaches in his highly informative book, *The Body Keeps the Score: Mind, Brain and Body in the Transformation of Trauma* [82].

The top-down approach involves improving our ability to notice our own state of mind, as we discussed in the previous chapter, and making conscious choices about where to place our attention and how to respond in any given situation. In other words, to engage the functions of the prefrontal cortex of the brain, which plays an important part in decision-making. Using this part of the brain, we can observe what's happening, analyse and predict the repercussions of our actions and consciously decide how to respond. Meditation and mindfulness techniques, including practices like yoga, can increase this focus and our ability to direct our attention. They can also raise awareness of bodily sensations and emotions, alerting us when we need to rebalance our nervous system [84]. Even taking a few moments to breathe deeply in a difficult situation can increase our ability to focus on issues. If we reach the point where we can pay attention in a crisis, and perhaps begin to plan, this in itself regulates the nervous system, because it stimulates production of dopamine, which (as we've discussed) improves alertness and feelings of optimism. That's why, in a crisis, having a plan or ticking off small tasks towards a greater goal can enable you to feel more positive and in control [77].

In tandem, the use of bottom-up approaches are ways of accessing the parasympathetic nervous system – our rest and digest mode – by physically changing how we move and relax to combat reactions to pressure. As well as enhancing top-down focus, yoga and deep breathing are also bottom-up approaches that can improve blood pressure and heart rate. They can reduce cortisol levels to counter the sympathetic system's accelerator effects, whilst also boosting the immune system [82]. Having a massage can also lower cortisol levels and increase the level of other neurochemicals such as serotonin and dopamine, which are useful in combating the effects of pressure [85].

Other ways of stimulating anti-stress neurochemicals

Giving ourselves a treat is a further means of producing the brain chemicals that are an antidote to stress. Dopamine production is stimulated by things that personally give us enjoyment, so it's important to find time for some of life's pleasures, even in the darkest of times. Eating and sleeping well and enjoying the outdoors can enhance our levels of the neurotransmitter serotonin – another neurochemical that supports positive moods and improves working memory. Aerobic exercise such as swimming, walking, running and cycling further help raise serotonin levels, as well as benefitting neuroplasticity and the growth of brain cells and neural pathways for new ways of thinking and acting [86].

In Chapter 6 we explored the positive effects of oxytocin on the nervous system in promoting empathy and trust. Studies have shown that positive social interactions increase levels of oxytocin and help suppress adverse threat responses. Having others around and finding time for social connections with people we trust, during tough times, can help us stay calm and decrease anxiety [87]. We'll come back to this in the *Advice* section further down.

We've seen the impact of existential threats on the autonomic nervous system. Functioning as a board during periods of crisis involves individual members noticing and managing their own stress reactions and well-being. And finding ways to focus and plan collectively to deal with the difficult task in front of them.

Advice on facing up to a doomsday scenario

Awareness: Accepting the impact of stress on your body and mind

In previous chapters we've advocated being aware of your thoughts, feelings, behaviour and surroundings. Here we look at the other piece of the jigsaw: being mindful of your stress responses and how they affect your body, so you can find the appropriate approach to maintaining your well-being, and boost your ability to handle a crisis with your board colleagues. This starts with being conscious of your usual response to pressure. When you receive a sudden shock, such as bad news, is your automatic, immediate response to fight, flight, freeze or flop? Do you experience a surge of energy in your body, feel a tired need to retreat and sleep or have a rabbit-in-the-headlights sense of frozen indecision? Also, if you are subject to unrelenting ongoing extreme pressure, how do you feel and what is your go-to learnt response to the actual or perceived threat? Where do you feel tension in your body, and what are your physical symptoms of illness, for example headaches, insomnia, skin or digestive disorders? Understanding how you react helps you to decide how to manage, pace and re-energise yourself.

ACE – Acknowledge, Connect and Engage

Several coaches suggested a technique called the *ACE approach*, which can help you access this kind of awareness and connect with your mind, emotions and body. It's used as part of Acceptance and Commitment Therapy, a practical, science-based approach for dealing with anxiety caused by a crisis. Originally created by the American psychologist Steven Hayes in the 1980s [88], it's been used, for instance, by the World Health Organisation to support refugees escaping conflict in Syria. Russ Harris, the author of the highly practical book *The Reality Slap: How to Survive and Thrive when Life Hits Hard* [88], describes the ACE approach as a way of anchoring yourself in an emotional storm. You're then in the position to analyse what's really going on and how best to act. The three ACE steps he describes follow below, and we've adapted them to the boardroom context. The stages can be practised regularly and reduced in terms of time-taken, so you can swiftly use them when you're experiencing pressure.

Acknowledge your thoughts and feelings

First, become curious about what is happening to you internally, by noticing the sensations in your body and the thoughts in your head. Without judgement, start to understand what's going on with you at this moment. To acknowledge these feelings and thoughts, name them to yourself by starting sentences, in the first person but in a detached way, with "*I'm noticing ...*" and "*I'm having ...*" Some examples of naming such feelings and thoughts might be "I'm noticing that my neck is stiff"; "I'm having thoughts about being confused"; "I'm noticing a memory of failing on a board before" and "I'm feeling tired and lacking in energy." You can adapt and change this according to what works for you. It's not about diverting these thoughts, rather it's about recognising they are there. By doing so, you will usually minimise some of their impact and feel calmer.

Connect with your body

At the same time begin to connect with your body and move it, to gain better control over your physical actions. For instance, you might do this by pressing your feet into the floor, sitting up straight and being aware of how you're sitting. Or by rotating your shoulders or opening your arms – moving your body in a way that works best for you. It's a matter of experimenting, being creative and adapting the movements to gently shift parts of your body. Continue acknowledging your thoughts and feelings, connecting with your body and then add the third step: engaging in what you are currently doing.

Engage in what you're doing

Really concentrate on what's happening in the moment. What do you see around you and what noises are you hearing? What do you smell or taste and what are you physically doing? This is to bring you back to concentrating on the here and now.

Practice this process so it takes just a few minutes and you can use it when you need it. For example, when you feel unable to concentrate because you are caught up in mentally cycling through the various ways in which the doomsday scenario might play out. You will still have accelerator and brake feelings, but exercises like this can reduce the impact and provide calmer and more engaged control.

Keeping your body and mind in balance

In addition to in-the-moment techniques, it's helpful to have a variety of other long-term approaches to ensure you remain healthy under pressure. This is about being mindful of what you and your colleagues need to do to remain resilient. An executive director in the energy sector recalled going through two doomsday scenarios in quick succession in his corporate life. In the first, a disgruntled minority shareholder tried to sue and close down a business, after his bid to take over the company was rebuffed. At the end of the experience, which lasted months, the executive felt close to mental breakdown. He realised "*I've always been a workaholic*" and didn't "*have any outside activities at all.*" This was a wake-up call and he decided to work with his wife to "*develop personal techniques for getting away from it and just have stuff outside [my] business life that I carried with me.*" Having learnt, from this early experience, the importance of looking after his mental and physical health, he felt better equipped when a second doomsday scenario hit in the early days of his next role.

The neuroscience and leadership researcher and consultant, David Rock, and his colleagues, refer to finding a combination of activities that help you to improve your well-being as your "healthy mind platter for optimal brain matter" [89]. Like choosing a good mix of foods to sustain our bodies, they argue that we need to select a healthy balance of activities to feed our brain and wider nervous system. The platter is a menu of activities which includes downtime, playing, sleeping, reflecting inwardly, focusing, exercising and connecting with others. We discussed the neuroscience behind the benefits of many of these in the *Psychological roots* section of this chapter. We recommend becoming aware of, and experimenting with, different mixes, to find which is the best one to help you withstand life's pressures. Let's look at the importance of one of these in particular: relating to others to bolster our resilience in times of crisis.

Crucial questions – Awareness

- What's my instinctive and my learnt response to pressure?
- What can I do at this very moment to energise or calm myself?
- What balance of activities outside of work will help me withstand longer-term pressure?

Relating: Seeking the comradery of colleagues

We've already mentioned that interacting and bonding with others can help relieve the stress triggered by a doomsday scenario. Socialising with colleagues in these circumstances can stimulate the production of oxytocin and support the balanced functioning of your autonomic nervous system. For instance, one study of a population of men in Sweden showed that there were fewer negative health outcomes, following stressful events, in men who had emotional support [90]. Being lonely at the top has real physiological implications. If you feel isolated, research indicates this promotes higher cortisol levels – likely to increase your stress responses – and you're less likely to sleep properly. All of which affects your ability to function well in the boardroom.

Through personal experience, our board interviewees found out how important social support was in a crisis. They spoke of the solace they found in having a network of colleagues they could confide in and socialise with, to help counter feelings of stress. Sometimes this was a small group of close colleagues whose brains they could pick or bounce ideas off. A CEO described when one private company, selling to the educational sector, was on the brink of going under because a credit crunch had led the government to cut the education budget. As sales and their share price plummeted, the CEO explained that it was vital to him that the non-executives all rallied round and were "*very supportive as they weathered the storm*." Key factors were attending all meetings together, contributing ideas and being positive about the executives finding a new investor to take over the business.

Other interviewees talked about the importance of having meals or a drink together. Socialising in some form, even amid the crisis, helped keep them sane. Ensuring that you find time to gather and mix with colleagues, during and after extremely tough situations, will help with the production of oxytocin and the brain chemicals that can counter stress. Some clients confess that they missed the comfort of "*the sense of sharedness*" once the doomsday situation had passed. Other interviewees recalled the importance of just having lighter, convivial moments as a respite from relentless pressure. A smile or a joke can relieve a situation, for instance, as it helps release endorphins, brain chemicals that relieve pain and stress and reduce cortisol build-up [91].

Crucial questions – Relating

- Where can I find social support inside or outside work?

Tactics: Reconnecting with your mission

Board members were acutely aware that in a doomsday scenario, despite all the chaos and pressure "*there was still a job to be done*." Interviewees talked about how helpful it was, at times of crisis, to go back to the core objectives of the organisation to achieve this. Getting through it all by continually returning to the question of "*what are we here to do?*" It's like the common purpose approach we discussed in Chapter 2. Thinking back to your roots, your organisation's reasons for existence, and keeping those front of mind. As we've seen already, having a goal releases substances like dopamine, which help counter the brain chemicals that induce feelings of stress.

A public sector CEO was in charge when a change in government policy meant their service for deprived communities was dismantled, and partly hived off to the private sector. They elaborated on the importance of holding onto their mission. They reflected that, within the organisation

> *there were long periods of time where people were literally hanging on by a thread. So the system felt very tense, very upset, very broken and as a board and a senior leadership team, we had to somehow hold that.*

They did so by homing in on the organisation's central purpose and remembering "*We're here to work with these people ... and the communities in which they live, who we've always worked with, and we have a passion about.*" Therefore, it was important to create something which enabled them, and their teams, to do "*the job that we valued and we loved.*" Even if it wasn't in the form that they had originally envisaged or wanted. Bearing that in mind, they ultimately were able to see that the change allowed "*a different set of opportunities and values to blossom.*"

Crucial questions – Tactics

• How can we use our purpose and mission to motivate and energise us in difficult times?

Focus and match your approach to the situation

As well as connecting with your passion and purpose to keep you going, board members also emphasised the importance of planning a crisis management strategy and being focused on its delivery. This involves taking advantage of good governance processes and practices to provide structure, by assessing and evaluating risks, planning a response, allocating roles and assigning resources. Paying attention to these things can engage the prefrontal cortex, a decision-making part of the brain, which, as we discussed earlier, can otherwise be inhibited by the brain chemicals released when we're stressed.

But in disaster situations, it's often difficult to know what to concentrate on first – where to start, let alone plan. To help decide what steps to take initially, David Snowden, a management consultant in complexity science, has developed a popular sense-making framework called Cynefin® (pronounced ku-nev-in). Its name comes from the Welsh word for "our multifaceted environment." It can be used by boards to analyse and understand the nature of the environment they're currently in, and decide how to proceed. Using a framework like this is like making a plan – it can regulate your nervous system and make you feel more in control. It's been used by a wide variety of commercial industries and institutions, such as the military and healthcare, and the European Commission promoted it to help those managing complexity and uncertainty during the Covid-19 pandemic. Other inspiring case studies of its wide-ranging application are vividly recounted in David Snowden's book, *Cynefin®: Weaving Sense-Making into the Fabric of our World* [92].

Power tool: Cynefin®

Environments found in nature are either predictable or unpredictable, and working out which you are in can help you to respond. Applying the Cynefin® framework helps boards to select their reaction in four very different contexts: clear, complicated, complex or chaotic – see Figure 7.1.

The first two – clear and complicated – are predictable contexts, where the situation is stable and ordered. In the clear environment, it's easy to work out the cause and effect of the situation and it's obvious what needs to be done. It's likely to be the type of problem that the board has met before (for example, a production problem is delaying deliveries and causing cash-flow problems). Here the best strategy is to make *sense* of the situation, by assessing and diagnosing the nature of the problem. Then you can *categorise* the issue into a type of problem you've

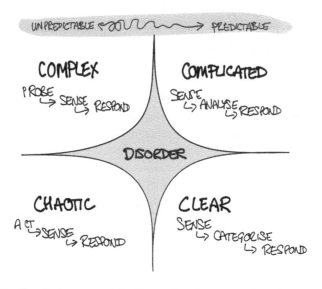

Figure 7.1 The Cynefin ® sense and decision-making framework for different environments

seen previously – for instance, a supply chain issue. You can then follow an already established process to *respond* in line with usual best practice – in this example, by looking for alternative suppliers.

On the other hand, if the cause of the problem is not immediately apparent, you may be in a complicated environment. For example, when an organisation is trying to market a service across a number of countries and geographies. Here the board needs to make *sense* of a situation which is multifaceted, by investigating it and collecting further data. Often this is done with the help of experts – in this instance with specialist knowledge of different regulatory regimes, competitors and potential client needs. Through this analysis, your possible options become more evident and assessing them reveals the best course of action. The reaction in this situation is likely to be *sense, analyse* and *respond.* You are following good practice, involving experts, whilst encouraging innovation and fresh thinking about how your product can be successful in a variety of target markets.

However, the work of boards, particularly those facing doomsday scenarios, is likely to take place in unpredictable contexts. Often a range of factors, like market conditions or unusual events, have come together in novel ways to cause uncertainty and disorder. Organisations can find it hard to recognise these unstable situations because people often assume "that a certain level of predictability and order exists in the world" [93]. Boards may be tempted to assume the best, particularly as they are usually observing everything from what Snowden describes as the disordered centre, with limited facts and information.

Recognising when you are in the third or fourth of the Cynefin® contexts – complex or chaotic – is key.

The hallmarks of a complex context are incomplete information on which to base decisions and outcomes which are uncertain. Politicians and the military are used to operating in this space – where answers are elusive, but the situation is stable enough for new ways of doing things to emerge. The Cynefin® framework advocates that the best strategy here is to first *probe* what's going on in the situation, then make *sense* and afterwards *respond.* This means experimenting with options to test out the environment, evaluating them, scaling up what's working and shutting down activities that lack positive impact. That way, you can gradually identify a sensible route forward.

The difficulties faced by our inside story family business lay within a complex environment. Their rapid experiments with new business models, partnerships and product development enabled them to probe their markets for feedback on what might work well, and make informed decisions based on emerging patterns in real-time data. They were operating according to Snowden's maxim that "Leaders who try to impose order in a complex context will fail, but those who set the stage, step back a bit, allow patterns to emerge, and determine which ones are desirable will succeed" [93].

The final and most difficult context is the chaotic situation, where it's impossible to work out the cause and effect of events and any reaction will be new. Events like a full-scale cyber attack or a tropical cyclone can cause a chaotic environment of utter disarray and seemingly random confusion. No patterns emerge to analyse, let alone solutions. Different and often counter-intuitive reactions are required in this highly unstable environment, and the board needs to stabilise the situation very quickly, so the first thing to do is *act* in a decisive way. If, for example, there's a cyber attack leading to a data breach of hospital patient records, the first act might be to authorise a system shutdown to prevent further breaches. The aim is to take one immediate step to try and establish a semblance of order. It doesn't have to be a perfect action and it certainly won't be a full plan, but you can make *sense* as further information emerges subsequently, once you've seen the repercussions of your action(s). In *response*, work on a clearer plan to move the situation to the complex context.

When using this framework, be aware that the way you choose to categorise the context can be influenced by your preferred leadership style. For example, you might decide it's a chaotic environment because you are an autocratic leader who likes to take decisive, unilateral action. Or that it's a complex context because you're a dynamic and entrepreneurial board which enjoys fast-paced experimentation. Flexible boards, CEOs and chairs take time to understand the nature of the context they work in and choose their style to match the context.

Crucial questions – Cynefin®

- What type of situation are we in?
- What does this mean for our first step?

Learning lessons

The Cynefin® framework involves sense-making in ways that suit the situation in which your board is operating. This aligns with the advice of our interviewees – to never underestimate the value of learning lessons during and after disastrous events. Many industries and organisations will use processes like *lessons learnt* exercises within their operations, but these can be overlooked at board level. A board consultant recommended using an agile approach, called after-action reviews, adopted by the US army and described in Marilyn Darling and colleagues' *Harvard Business Review* article, *Learning in the Thick of It* [94]. Like other lessons learnt exercises, after-action reviews are a way of capturing good practice for further use, and identifying mistakes to avoid repeating them. But the difference is that they take place at regular intervals during the current crisis, rather than during a review of the catastrophe once it's concluded. The process includes "tight feedback cycles" of regular, short, action-review meetings to put learning into practice in real time. It also involves logging and tracking the impact of decisions, and giving the board feedback on what's successful, can be used again, or should be avoided. This helps boards use immediate experience to make sense of their situation and improve decisions about what action to take next. In a doomsday context, the key is that the chair or CEO must make sure that regular lesson reviews take place, so they become habitual, like the daily meetings in our inside story.

Once the crisis is over, there's a temptation to skip further reflection and move on to the next challenge. To do this is to miss learning from the experience. One charity chair was insistent on instigating a lessons learnt process with the board after a humanitarian charity had been put into voluntary liquidation when funding dried up. They'd led many similar reviews in their corporate career and they shared their blueprint. The chair, or an external consultant, interviews all the board members separately about what happened in the crisis and why. They make it clear that the purpose is to understand what happened, rather than attach blame and responsibility. Importantly, these conversations are confidential, and acknowledge the emotional side of the experience for board members.

They focus on finding out what went so wrong and why, ask whether this could have been avoided by a different approach, and if so, what kind? In trying to draw out what can be learnt from experience, to apply in the future, they focus on specific actions, policies and procedures that contributed to the crisis. This includes failures to read the warning signs and the general culture of the organisation and the board, including governance issues. They identify things that went well (which individuals and the organisation can be proud of) and consider repeating them in the future. They also consider unforeseen events, including the actions and decisions of third parties, over which the organisation had little or no control. Finally, the chair or interviewer reports the interview summary themes to the board for debate, identifying learnings and agreeing next steps.

Crucial questions – Tactics

- What can we learn from how we've managed this crisis so far, to guide our next step?
- How do we make sure this learning is of practical benefit and not forgotten?

Summary

The physical and mental impact of extreme pressure

When catastrophe strikes it can be all consuming in time and energy, and requires a different approach from boards. Individual board members' psychological and physiological reactions and coping mechanisms can vary greatly, and be different from their responses in calmer times.

Your possible range of responses

Some board members fight back by going beyond the call of duty, whilst others may act unethically for self-preservation. You may also see colleagues withdraw from the doomsday threat, either physically or mentally – becoming inactive and unable to respond (or even falling ill).

The role of your nervous system

When you feel threatened in a crisis, neuroscience tells us that instinctive and learnt reactions are triggered in your brain, neural pathways and the rest of your nervous system. These result in short-term acute stress or longer-term chronic stress, which can impact your health and well-being immediately or over time. This can be relieved by activities that encourage the release of anti-stress neurochemicals.

Awareness: Manage the impact of stress on your body

Concentrating on how you're feeling and what's happening to you physically at any given moment can help you recognise and manage your immediate response to stress. You can counter the effects of continuous pressure by consciously choosing a healthy diet, adequate sleep and activities such as regular exercise and mindfulness.

Relating: Seek the comradery of colleagues

Socialising and enjoying lighter moments with colleagues and others will release brain chemicals that relieve anxiety.

Tactics: Focus and match your approach to the situation

Focusing on your ultimate vision and goals, and continually learning lessons during and after the event, creates new neural pathways and increases your capacity to adapt. It also helps produce the brain chemicals that are antidotes to extreme stress.

Power tool: The Cynefin® framework

This sense-making framework aids your understanding of your environment. Disasters are often complex or chaotic contexts, and your board needs to decide which approach is needed to instil some order and find the best way forward.

Further reading

The Reality Slap: How to Survive and Thrive when Life Hits Hard by Russ Harris.

The Body Keeps the Score: Mind, Brain and Body in the Transformation of Trauma by Bessel van der Kolk.

How to Have a Good Day: The Essential Toolkit for a Productive Day at Work and Beyond by Caroline Webb.

Chapter 8

Board relationships in the future

Self-defence in the boardroom

Throughout this book, we've seen how boardroom pressures can lead us to behave in irrational and sometimes unhelpful ways towards colleagues, to protect ourselves. These are reactions to sharing power with people who have different personalities and approaches, and to the demands of the constantly changing environment in which we work and live. We've looked at seven tricky dynamics for boards – situations in which interpersonal relationships are impeding the group's ability to focus on the task in hand. We've explored how different aspects of psychology can help us understand the causes of defensiveness and manage our stress responses more effectively.

We've discussed explanations from psychodynamic psychologists for seesaw power dynamics between executives and non-executives, for conflict which hardens into a stand-off and for the tyranny of bullies on boards. They describe psychological defence mechanisms, shaped by your early life experiences, and triggered when you work alongside others in high-stakes situations; for example, in board meetings during which you need to hold power together, and make decisions which impact the organisation and other people. These situations can lead you to protect yourself from uncomfortable feelings by falling back on approaches from your early years, displacing your emotions, and leaning into the pack instincts of the group.

We've also explored insights of cognitive behavioural psychologists into ways that boards can become cut off from their operating environment and responsibilities. How they distance themselves physically and mentally to avoid reality, ignoring things or failing to be curious. How they become cowed into rubber stamping decisions made elsewhere, or complacently detached from their organisations and markets. These psychologists outline how reward and punishment in your environment shapes your behaviour, and how you might be tempted to navigate the challenges of highly complex environments by taking an easy path. Finally, we've looked at how your mind and body influence you in the boardroom, especially

DOI: 10.4324/9780429340239-12

when working with people from whom you are different, and during catastrophic situations. Findings from neuroscience reveal the sensitivity of your nervous system to discomfort and threat, and the diverse and divisive impact of your physiological survival-based responses on your thoughts, feelings and actions.

The common themes across these scenarios and schools of psychology are that difficulty, discomfort and feelings of threat or jeopardy can lead you to deploy self-protective defences. Measures which can have the unfortunate side-effects of limiting your individual capacity for judicious action and undermining your ability to relate well to your colleagues. You are likely to have limited awareness of these reactions because they often arise unconsciously or automatically. These are the roots of difficult relationship dynamics on boards, which are often invisible to the people involved.

Boards under increasing pressure

Our interconnected world is changing rapidly, bringing great opportunity for board members. It also brings increased stress, which is likely to trigger defensive reactions and complex dynamics. The backdrop of global warming, digital upheaval, geopolitical and financial uncertainty – from wars, pandemics, cyber attacks, viral misinformation and climate-related events – heightens the uncertainty associated with board work.

Business today is no longer just about profit, but about the impact on planet, people and communities. Stakeholder expectations about ESG standards put pressure on boards to direct their organisations in more ethical and sustainable ways. Overcoming new regulatory hurdles can be a taxing endeavour for board members who lack in-depth sector knowledge. New business models – triple bottom line, products-to-services, virtual business, circular economy – are key to tackling these issues. Balancing these competing aspects, under the close scrutiny of diverse stakeholders, brings new tensions into the boardroom.

Across all sectors, public opinion, by nature fickle and unpredictable, is an ever-present source of threat. Social media puts boards under the spotlight and can open the door to attacks (sometimes unfounded) on the credibility and integrity of organisations or individuals. These shifts can gather instant strength and momentum, making reputation management a real concern.

Understanding the opportunities of tech innovation – increased communication, productivity and environmental protection – will enhance board performance, but the risks are an ongoing challenge. Getting to grips with emerging fields like quantum computing, artificial intelligence, blockchain, Web3 and the metaverse, requires a level of digital savviness which many board members simply don't have, leaving them feeling ill-equipped and exposed. Cyber security can be a particular source of anxiety, including concerns about data theft or ransomware targeting day-to-day operations.

Increasing diversity in the boardroom brings the need to communicate and collaborate with those who are different from you. This creates scope for misunderstanding and tension around the table. It's a particular hazard for boards which can't see the real opportunity to promote inclusive behaviour – one which will pay long-term dividends.

The antidote: The ART of boardroom relationships

Pressures on your board are increasing, which is likely to heighten defensive reactions from members, and raise the prospect of difficult relationship dynamics. But we've shown in this book how practising the ART of managing board relationships can counteract these problems. We've outlined how your capacity for self-awareness, conscious choice and bonding with others in collaborative groups gives you the power to lessen defensive effects. And the good news is that boards with collaborative and constructive cultures can harness their members' talents and insights to make better decisions.

What does this mean for boards in the future? Effective boards will recruit members who can operate with a high level of awareness of themselves, others and their environment, and use this to fuel personal and professional development. Individuals who can continually rewire their own brains through active engagement with experiences, ideas and people around them, will be increasingly valuable on boards. This is because they can adapt and grow to meet the challenges and opportunities surrounding them. We also predict that the capacity to use this awareness to relate well to others and manage relationships will be an ever more vital and differentiating skill, because it can liberate board members from distracting dynamics. We believe that board members will need a kitbag of tactics to deal with the inevitable uncomfortable relationships thrown up by working together in an increasingly stressful environment.

Let's review in more detail the capabilities of the ART of managing boardroom relationships and how boards might benefit from these in the future.

Awareness

This involves noticing your own contribution to a situation and identifying options for managing your defensive reactions. It also means developing insights into your own mindset, beliefs and assumptions – the stories you tell yourself about what's happening, and the limitations of your perspective and thought patterns. It means nurturing the ability to tune into the ways that your physiological responses to discomfort and threat affect your thoughts, feelings, and actions, in the moment and over the long run.

New generations are a valuable source of different kinds of awareness on boards. We've seen this with millennials, born between 1981 and 1996. Research suggests that people in this age group are typically committed to sustainable development goals, including equality, sustainability, peace, justice and poverty reduction. Members of this and future generations can elevate your board's awareness of social and environmental issues, and commitment to governance tenets like diversity, equity and inclusion. Generation Z – digital natives born roughly between 1995 to 2010 – also offer new levels of tech insight, potentially opening up new horizons for your organisation [95]. And who knows what Generation Alpha, born into the 21st century after 2010, might have in store for boardrooms in the future?

Relating

When you are equipped with some awareness of yourself and others, you can seek to understand your board colleagues and make conscious decisions about how best to relate to them. You can proactively seek and maintain alignment, clarify mutual expectations and hold each other accountable, and build relationships beyond the board, down into the organisation and out into markets and partners. Fundamentally, you can start using your board colleagues as a vital resource of challenge and support, so that as a group you are far more than the sum of your individual parts.

We're optimistic about the capability of humans to remain flexible, resilient and innovative in finding ways to work well together in a changing world. Our research revealed examples of board members from all generations with an intuitive sense of how to manage relationships well. And evidence suggests a trend towards millennials and Generation Z leaders being even more interested in understanding how others tick [95]. They are open to the ways in which psychology can help unlock some of the mysteries of our behaviour and understand each other in stressful boardroom situations. More and more, management schools and commercial programmes for aspiring board members are not only covering practical topics, like strategy, governance and managing risk, but also the psychology of leadership. We think a basic grounding in the dynamics of human relationships will become an essential element on every board level educational syllabus. We believe those who can apply this knowledge effectively, to themselves and their board relationships, will boost the performance of their boards and organisations.

Tactics

We've shared a selection of tactics from board veterans and their advisors for responding to each of the boardroom dynamics mentioned in the previous chapters. They comprise a wide range of tools and models, including for gathering information and resources and establishing ground rules and roles. They're also ideal for promoting thinking, communication, sense- and decision-making and creating safe spaces for discussion, adaptation and learning lessons.

We suggest that a crucial area for boards to develop tactics in the future is to make smart use of online communication channels. The Covid-19 pandemic catapulted many boards from traditional face-to-face meetings into entirely virtual meetings, which came more naturally to some generations and sectors than others. Understanding the optimum hybrid mix for your board, and how best to work in different environments, is vital for effective interaction. This means paying attention to situations where relationships will benefit from live meetings and working out what tasks are best done when physically together. It also means understanding how virtual meetings and digital chat channels can keep you connected, responsive to emerging situations and able to act fast when needed.

Practising and honing the ART of managing boardroom relationship dynamics is an ongoing process. We trust this book will serve as a useful guide and leave the last word to our interviewees.

Epilogue

A last word on your board relationships

In writing this book, we are very grateful to the many board members and board advisors who have contributed by sharing their stories of the board dynamics they've encountered. We hope we've conveyed their wise counsel about managing the secret life of boards, and that you will benefit from their practical guidance.

During our interviews we asked each person to summarise what advice they would give their younger self, and their reflections sum up the spirit of the ART of boardroom relationship dynamics. Their advice is to focus on human elements and this reflects many of the themes we've covered in this book. It feels fitting to end by sharing their pragmatic answers – the last word in fostering healthy boards and organisations now and in years to come.

- *Recruit for board roles with character in mind.* Look for colleagues who are flexible, inquisitive, self-aware, able to respect and appreciate others and resilient in the face of pressure.
- *Build trust.* Get to know each other personally – spend time together and have conversations beyond your board work. This pays great dividends in tough times.
- *Listen with patience.* Discussions take time, and good decisions can take a while to percolate. Listen to colleagues and give processes time to work through.
- *Be thoughtful and courageous in your interventions.* Think deeply, then speak your mind with courage – don't let fear of conflict or looking foolish hold you back.
- *Be curious and keep learning.* An open, interested mind will keep you adaptable and able to learn and develop throughout your career, and help you relate well to colleagues.
- *Show your human side.* Don't hide who you are. Boards really come alive when people bring human qualities like empathy, vulnerability and humour to the table.

DOI: 10.4324/9780429340239-13

References

1. Harvey Nash (2020) *The Alumni/Harvey Nash Board Report*. London: London Business School Leadership Institute, p. 10.
2. Kets de Vries, M.F.R., Korotov, K. and Florent-Treacy, E. (2016) *Coach and couch: The psychology of making better leaders*. 2nd edition. Basingstoke, Hampshire: Palgrave Macmillan.
3. Obholzer, A., Roberts, V.Z. and Tavistock Clinic (1994) *Consulting to institutions, the unconscious at work: Individual and organizational stress in the human services*. London: Routledge, p. 44.
4. Freud, S., Strachey, J., Freud, A., Rothgeb, C. and Richards, A. (1953) *The standard edition of the complete psychological works of Sigmund Freud*. London: Hogarth Press.
5. Freud, A. and Baines, C. (1937) *The ego and the mechanisms of defence*. London: Hogarth.
6. Freud, S., Ragg-Kirkby, H. and Bowie, M. (2003) *An outline of psychoanalysis (Penguin modern classics)*. London: Penguin Books.
7. Jaques, E. (1998) *Requisite organization: A total system for effective managerial organization and managerial leadership for the 21st century*. Rev. second edition. Arlington, VA: Cason Hall.
8. Stamp, G.P. and Brunel Institute of Organisation and Social Studies (1988) *Longitudinal research into methods of assessing managerial potential*. Uxbridge: Brunel Institute of Organisation and Social Studies.
9. Costa, P.T. and McCrae, R.R. (1992) 'Four ways five factors are basic', *Personality and Individual Differences*, 3(6), pp. 653–665.
10. Burgo, J. (2012) *Why do I do that?: Psychological defense mechanisms and the hidden ways they shape our lives*. Chapel Hill, NC: New Rise Press.
11. Schein, E.H. and Bennis, W.G. (1965) *Personal and organisational change through group methods: The laboratory approach*. New York: John Wiley & Son.
12. Edmondson, A.C. (2019) *The fearless organization: Creating psychological safety in the workplace for learning, innovation, and growth*. Hoboken, NJ: Wiley, p. 8.
13. ReWork with Google (2016) *Tool: Foster psychological safety*. Available at: https://rework.withgoogle.com/guides/understanding-team-effectiveness/steps/foster-psychological-safety (Accessed: 12 December 2022).
14. Klein, M. (2002) *Love, guilt, and reparation, and other works, 1921–1945*. New York: Free Press.
15. Bion, W.R. (1961) *Experiences in groups, and other papers*. London: Tavistock Publications, p. 53.

16. Rioch, M. (1971) 'All we like sheep (Isaiah 53:6): Followers and leaders', *Psychiatry*, 34(3), pp. 258–273.

17. Shenk, J.W. (2014) *Powers of two: Finding the essence of innovation in creative pairs*. London: Eamon Dolan.

18. Berger, J.G., Johnston, K. and ProQuest (2015) *Simple habits for complex times: Powerful practices for leaders*. Stanford, CA: Stanford Business Books.

19. Covey, S.R. (2004) *The 7 habits of highly effective people*. New edition. London: Simon & Schuster, p. 239.

20. Heifetz, R.A. and Linsky, M. (2017) *Leadership on the line: Staying alive through the dangers of leading*. Boston, MA: Harvard Business School Press, p. 2.

21. Whitney, C.R. (1991) 'Robert Maxwell, 68: From refugee to the ruthless builder of a publishing empire', *New York Times*, 6th November. Available at: Robert Maxwell, 68: From refugee to the ruthless builder of a publishing empire – The New York Times (nytimes.com) (Accessed: 11th December 2022).

22. Preston, J. (2020) *Fall: The mystery of Robert Maxwell*. London: Penguin Books.

23. Milmo, D. (2001) 'DTI slams Kevin Maxwell and Goldman Sachs', *The Guardian*, 30th March. Available at: DTI slams Kevin Maxwell and Goldman Sachs | Newspapers & magazines | The Guardian (Accessed: 11th December 2022).

24. Acas (2021) *If you're treated unfairly at work – Being bullied*. Available at: https://www.acas.org.uk/if-youre-treated-unfairly-at-work/being-bullied (Accessed: 10th May 2022).

25. Einarsen, S., Skogstad, A. and Glasø, L. (2013) 'When leaders are bullies: Concepts, antecedents, and consequences', in Skipton Leonard, H., Lewis, R., Freedman, A.M. and Passmore, J. (eds) *The Wiley Blackwell handbook of the psychology of leadership, change and organisational development*. Hoboken, NJ: Wiley Blackwell.

26. Kets de Vries, M.F.R. and Miller, D. (1984) *The neurotic organization*. The Jossey-Bass management series. San Francisco: Jossey-Bass.

27. Babiak, P. and Hare, R.D. (2007) *Snakes in suits: When psychopaths go to work*. London: HarperCollins.

28. Latané, B. and Darley, J.M. (1968) 'Group inhibition of bystander intervention in emergencies', *Journal of Personal Social Psychology*, 10(3), pp. 215–221.

29. Financial Services Authority (2011) *The failure of the Royal Bank of Scotland*, in Financial Services Authority board report, para 608. Available at: The failure of the Royal Bank of Scotland: Financial Services Authority board report (fca.org.uk) (Accessed: 11th December 2022).

30. Berne, E. (1964) *Games people play: The psychology of human relationships*. New York: Grove Press.

31. Stewart, I. and Joines, V. (2012) *TA today: A new introduction to transactional analysis*. Second edition. Melton Mowbray: Lifespace Publishing.

32. Karpman, S. (1968) 'Fairy tales and script drama analysis', *Transactional Analysis Bulletin*, 7(26), pp. 39–43. Available at: https://karpmandramatriangle.com/pdf/DramaTriangle.pdf (Accessed: 11th December 2022).

33. Boston, R. and Ellis, K. (2019) *Upgrade: Building your capacity for complexity*. London: LeaderSpace.

34. Emerald, D. (2016) *The power of TED* (*The Empowerment Dynamic)®*. 10th anniversary edition. Bainbridge Island, WA: Polaris Publishing.

35. Dethmer, J., Chapman, D. and Klemp, K. (2014) *The 15 commitments of conscious leadership: A new paradigm for sustainable success.* United States: Conscious Leadership Group.
36. Larcker, D.F. and Miles, S.A. (2010) *2010 survey on CEO succession planning.* Available at: 2010 CEO Succession Planning Survey | Stanford Graduate School of Business (Accessed: 11th December 2022).
37. Skinner, B.F. (1971) *Beyond freedom and dignity.* London: Penguin, p. 20.
38. Pavlov, I.P. and Anrep, G.V. (trans. and ed.) (1927) *Conditioned reflexes: An investigation of the physiological activity of the cerebral cortex.* Oxford, UK: Oxford University Press.
39. Gray, P. (2011) *Psychology.* Sixth edition. New York: Worth, pp. 108–109.
40. Seligman, M.E.P. (2006) *Learned optimism: How to change your mind and your life.* New York: Vintage Books, p. 319.
41. Seligman, M.E.P. and Maier, S.F. (1967) 'Failure to escape traumatic shock', *Journal of Experimental Psychology*, 74(1), pp. 1–9.
42. Pattakos, A. (2008) *Prisoners of our thoughts: Viktor Frankl's principles for discovering meaning in life and work.* San Francisco, CA: Berrett-Koehler, p. 194.
43. Bandura, A. (2001) 'Social cognitive theory: An agentic perspective', *Annual Review of Psychology*, 52, pp. 1–26.
44. Charan, R. (2005) *Boards that deliver: Advancing corporate governance from compliance to competitive advantage.* San Francisco, CA : Wiley.
45. Ellis, A. (1994) *Reason and emotion in psychotherapy. Revised and updated edition.* New York: Birch Lane Press.
46. Steiner, I.D. (1972) *Group process and productivity.* New York: Academic Press.
47. Heffernan, M. (2019) *Wilful blindness: Why we ignore the obvious.* New edition. London: Simon & Schuster, p. 32, 7.
48. Bandura, A., Caprara, G. and Zsolnai, L. (2000) 'Corporate transgressions through moral disengagement', *Journal of Human Values*, 6(1), pp. 57–64.
49. Wells, G.H., Horwitz, J. and Seetharaman, D. (2021) '"Facebook knows instagram is toxic for many teen girls, company documents show" in "The Facebook files – a Wall Street journal investigation"', *Wall Street Journal*. Available at: https://www.wsj.com/articles/the-facebook-files-11631713039 (Accessed: 15th December 2022).
50. Kahneman, D. (2012) *Thinking, fast and slow.* London: Penguin, p. 255, 201, 305 and 13.
51. Thaler, R.H. and Sunstein, C.R. (2009) *Nudge: Improving decisions about health, wealth and happiness.* Revised and expanded edition. New York: Penguin.
52. Tversky, A. and Kahneman, D. (1974) 'Judgment under uncertainty: Heuristics and biases', *Science*, 185(4157), pp. 1124–1131.
53. Busenitz, L.W. and Barney, J.B. (1997) 'Differences between entrepreneurs and managers in large organisations: Biases and heuristics in strategic decision-making', *Journal of Business Venturing*, 12, pp. 9–30.
54. Gewirtz, J.L. and Kurtines, W.M. (1991) *Handbook of moral behavior and development: Volume 1: Theory.* Hillsdale, NJ: L. Erlbaum, p. 87.
55. Bandura, A. (2016) *Moral disengagement: How people do harm and live with themselves.* New York: Worth Publishers.
56. White, J., Bandura, A. and Bero, L. (2009) 'Moral disengagement in the corporate world', *Accountability in Research*, 16(1), pp. 1–55.

57. Bandura, A. and Walters, R.H. (1963) *Social learning and personality development*. New York: Holt, Rinehart & Winston.

58. Harvard Business Review (2013) *HBR guide to project management*. HBR Guide Series. Boston: Harvard Business Review Press.

59. Yu, H. and Bower, J. (2009) 'Taking a "Deep Dive": What only a top leader can do', *Harvard Business School Working Papers*. Boston: Harvard Business School, p. 2.

60. Kelley, T. and Littman, J. (2001) *The art of innovation*. New York: Doubleday.

61. Sharpe, B. (2020) *Three horizons 2020: The patterning of hope*. Second revised edition. London: Triarchy Press.

62. Krogerus, M., Tschäppeler, R. and Piening, J. (2018) *The decision book: Fifty models for strategic thinking*. New fully revised ed. New York: W. W. Norton & Company.

63. Barrett, L.F. (2017) *How emotions are made: The secret life of the brain*. Boston: Houghton Mifflin Harcourt, p. 239.

64. Collins, A.M. and Loftus, E.F. (1975) 'A spreading-activation theory of semantic processing', *Psychological Review*, (82), pp. 407–428.

65. DeYoung, C.G., Carey, B.E., Krueger, R.F. and Ross, S.R. (2016) 'Ten aspects of the big five in the personality inventory for DSM-5', *Personality Disorders: Theory, Research, and Treatment*, 7(2), pp. 113–123.

66. Weill, P., Apel, T., Woerner, S.L. and Banner, J.S. (2019) 'It pays to have a digitally savvy board', *MIT Sloan Management Review* (Spring 2019). Available at: https://sloanreview.mit.edu/article/it-pays-to-have-a-digitally-savvy-board (Accessed: 18 December 2022).

67. Women on Boards and Proviti (2022) *Hidden truth 2022: Board diversity in the FTSE all-share ex350*. Available at: https://www.womenonboards.net/womenonboards-AU/media/AU-PDFs/WoB_The-Hidden-Truth-22_FINAL.pdf (Accessed: 18 December 2022).

68. Syed, M. (2020) *Rebel ideas: The power of diverse thinking*. London: John Murray.

69. Johnson, S.K., Hekman, D.R. and Chan, E.T. (2016) 'If there's only one woman in your candidate pool, there's statistically no chance she will be hired', *Harvard Business Review* (2016, April).

70. Post, C., Lokshin, B. and Boone, C. (2021) 'Research: Adding women to the C-suite changes how companies think', *Harvard Business Review* (2021, April).

71. Hebb, D.O. (1949) *The organisation of behaviour*. New York: Wiley.

72. Barrett, L.F. (2021) *Seven and a half lessons about the brain*. London: Picador.

73. O'Connor, J.A. and Lages, A. (2019) *Coaching the brain: Practical applications of neuroscience to coaching*. London: Routledge, pp. 19–20.

74. LeDoux, J. (2015) *Anxious: The modern mind in the age of anxiety*. London: Oneworld Publications.

75. Casey, M.E. and Murphy Robinson, S. (2017) *The neuroscience of inclusion: New skills for new times*. Denver, CO: Outskirts Press, pp. 39, 65 and 8.

76. Arnsten, A.F.T. (2009) 'Stress signalling pathways that impair prefrontal cortex structure and function', *National Review of Neuroscience*, 10(6), pp. 410–422.

77. Sawaguchi, T. and Goldman-Rakic, P.S. (1991) 'D1 dopamine receptors in pre-frontal cortex: Involvement in working memory', *Science*, 251, pp. 947–951.

78. Swart, T., Chisholm, K. and Brown, P. (2015) *Neuroscience for leadership: Harnessing the brain gain advantage*. London: Palgrave Macmillan UK.

79. Zak, P.J. (2013) *Moral molecule: How trust works*. New York: Penguin Group.

80. Creary, S.J., McDonnell, M., Ghai, S. and Scruggs, J. (2019) 'When and why diversity improves your board's performance', *Harvard Business Review* (March, 2019). Available at: https://hbr.org/2019/03/when-and-why-diversity-improves-your-boards-performance (Accessed: 18 December 2022).

81. Hofstede, G. (2001) *Culture's consequences: Comparing values, behaviors, institutions and organizations across nations.* Thousand Oaks, CA: Sage.

82. Van der Kolk, B.A. (2014) *The body keeps the score: Mind, brain and body in the transformation of trauma.* New York: Viking.

83. Brann, A. (2017) *Neuroscience for coaches: How to use the latest insights for the benefit of your clients.* Second edition. London, Philadelphia: Kogan Page.

84. Pal, G., Velkumary, S. and Madanmohan (2004) 'Effect of short-term practice of breathing exercises on autonomic functions in normal human volunteers', *Indian Journal of Medical Research*, 120(2), pp. 115–121.

85. Field, T., Hernandez-Reif, M., Diego, M., Schanberg, S. and Kuhn, C. (2005) 'Cortisol decreases and serotonin and dopamine increase following massage therapy', *International Journal of Neuroscience*, 115(10), pp. 1397–1413.

86. Xie, Y., Wu, Z., Sun, L., Zhou, L., Wang, G., Xiao, L. and Wang, H. (2021) 'The effects and mechanisms of exercise on the treatment of depression', *Frontiers in Psychiatry*, 12, p. 705559.

87. Heinrichs, M.B., Kirschbaum, T. and Ehlert, U.C. (2004) 'Social support and oxytocin interact to suppress cortisol and subjective responses to psychosocial stress', *Biological Psychiatry*, 54(12), pp. 1389–1398.

88. Harris, R. (2021) *The reality slap: How to survive and thrive when life hits hard.* Second edition. London: Robinson.

89. Poelmans, S.A.Y., Rock, D., Siegel, D.J. and Payne, J.D. (2012) 'The healthy mind platter', *Neuroleadership Journal*, (4), pp. 1–23, p. 3.

90. Rosengren, A., Orth-Gomér, K., Wedel, H. and Wilhelmsen, L. (1993) 'Stressful life events, social support, and mortality in men born in 1933', *BMJ* (Clinical Research edition), (307), pp. 1102–5.

91. Panksepp, J. and Burgdorf, J. (2003) '"Laughing" rats and the evolutionary antecedents of human joy?' *Physiology & Behavior*, 79(3), pp. 533–547.

92. Snowden, D., Greenberg, R. and Bertsch, B. (2021) *Cynefin® weaving sense-making into the fabric of our world.* Singapore: Cognitive Edge - The Cynefin Co.

93. Snowden, D.J. and Boone, M.E. (2007) 'A leader's framework for decision making', *Harvard Business Review*, 85(11), pp. 68–76.

94. Darling, M., Parry, C. and Moore, J. (2005) 'Learning in the thick of it', *Harvard Business Review*, 83(7), pp. 84–92.

95. Cheng, M. (2019) '8 characteristics of millennials that support sustainable development goals (SDGs)', *Forbes* (online). Available at: https://www.forbes.com/sites/margueritacheng/2019/06/19/8-characteristics-of-millennials-that-support-sustainable-development-goals-sdgs/?sh=3ceb34e329b7 (Accessed: 18 December 2022).

Index